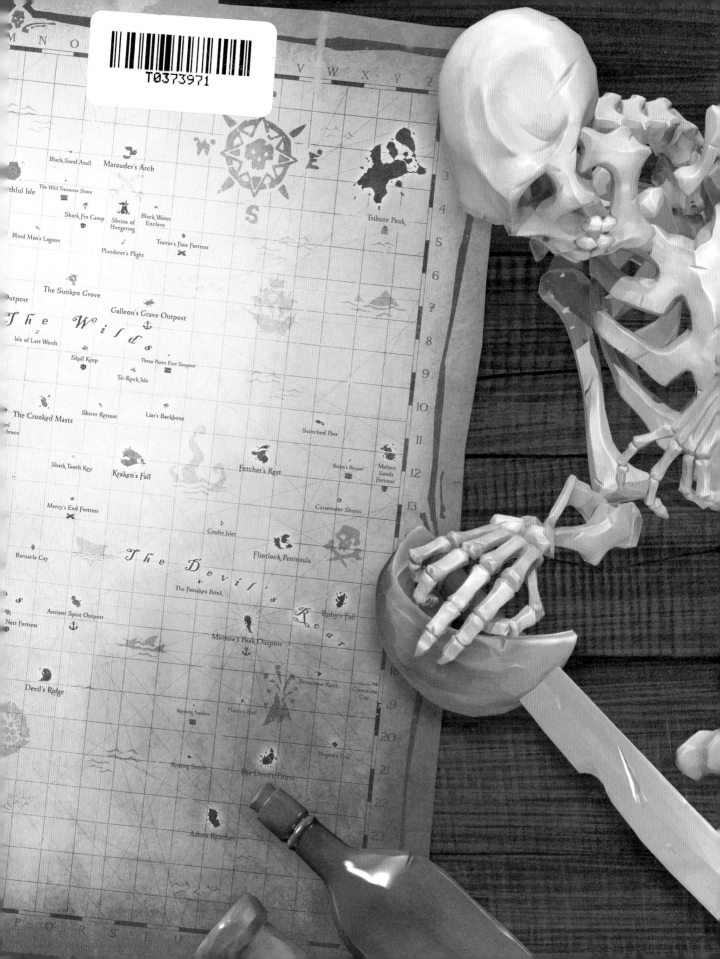

M N O P Q R S T U V W X Y Z

Black Sand Atoll   Marauder's Arch   3

thful Isle   The Wild Treasures Store   4

Shark Fin Camp   Black Water   Tribute Peak
                       Enclave
Blind Man's Lagoon   Shrine of   5
                      Hungering   Traitor's Fate Fortress
              Plunderer's Plight

                                                                             6
        The Sunken Grove
Outpost   7
            Galleon's Grave Outpost
The Wilds
                                                                             8
 Isle of Last Words

        Skull Keep   Three Paces East Seapost   9
            Tri-Rock Isle

                                                                            10
The Crooked Masts   Shiver Retreat   Liar's Backbone
brace
                                        Scatched Pass   11

    Shark Tooth Key   Fetcher's Rest   Brian's Bazaar   Molten 12
        Kraken's Fall   Sands
                                                                           Fortress

    Mercy's End Fortress   Cursewater Shores   13

                    Cinder Islet
Barnacle Cay   The Devil's   Flintlock Peninsula

                The Forsaken Brink
                                            R o a r   Ruby's Fall
Nest Fortress   Ancient Spire Outpost
                        Morrow's Peak Outpost

Devil's Ridge   18
                            Brimstone Rock   Glowstone
                                                Cay   19
            Roaring Traders   Flame's End
                                                                           20

                                        Magma's Tide   21
        Roaring Sands   The Devil's Thrust
                                                                           22

        Ashen Reaches   23

P Q R S T U

Sea of thieves

The COOKBOOK

Sea of Thieves
The COOKBOOK

ISBN: 9781803365077

Published by
Titan Books
A division of Titan Publishing Group Ltd
144 Southwark St
London
SE1 0UP

www.titanbooks.com

FIRST EDITION: MARCH 2024
2 4 6 8 10 9 7 5 3

DID YOU ENJOY THIS BOOK?
We love to hear from our readers. Please e-mail us at:
readerfeedback@titanemail.com or write to Reader Feedback at the above address.

To receive advance information, news, competitions, and exclusive offers online, please sign up for the Titan newsletter on our website: www.titanbooks.com

A CIP catalogue record for this title is available from the British Library.

Printed and bound in China.

GUIDE TO SYMBOLS IN RECIPES

 Difficulty level

 Preparation and cooking times

 Yield or servings

 Dietary information

KAYCE BAKER

TITANBOOKS

CONTENTS

HEY THERE PIRATE!

I need a very, very large drink, or maybe just a very, very good meal. One that I can enjoy while recounting the tale of how I, Larinna, landed here in the Sea of Thieves. I can share the story of that fateful morning as I woke to the heavenly smell of bacon and eggs and was eternally grateful that the tavern-keeper was willing to feed me in exchange for my stowaway tale. It has always been that meal I think of fondly and one that piqued my curiosity about the cuisine I was to encounter on my travels. After all, a pirate cannot live on grog alone, no matter how hard we try.

Quite a while ago, on a brisk, clear evening, a confident pirate with a captain's swagger strolled into The George and Kraken professing to be "Chef Hendrick, fine-dining pioneer to discerning crews and author of several of the best-selling journals on how to cook!" Oh, he was an arrogant sort, the kind of pirate I like, the kind that will never scuttle or turn over a ship. But he was here to talk about food, ingredients, and the mastery of cooking, for which he had a passion and was prepared to share with the tavern-keeper. I overheard all of it.

The tale goes that Merrick and his wife Serik founded The Hunter's Call, a Trading Company that runs its business out of Sea Posts all throughout the Sea of Thieves, trading in fish, meat, and fruits. Hendrick, Merrick's brother, was also recruited into the family business. Hendrick, however, had a vision, a plan, a dream to start a culinary empire. He fancied a Chef Hendrick's dining hall at every outpost, a sail-through galley at each Sea Post, and even a travelling kitchen that would call in at the Glorious Sea Dog Tavern and the Tavern of Legends. Oh, he rattled off some tantalizing recipes, like twice-boiled Black Scaled Snake Tail infused with coconut, served on Rum-Smashed Potatoes with a side of Wilted Palm Leaves, or Grog-Soaked Bristled Pig Legs, which comes with crispy Parrot Feathers and a Skeleton Bone Marrow Broth.

Although his dream was grand, Hendrick's passion and ambition to bring gourmet cuisine to the Sea of Thieves outweighed his resources to be sure, and so he set sail, on a culinary adventure of legendary measure, to visit each tavern across the seas and teach every tavern-keeper the skills necessary to elevate their cuisine. Chef Hendrick remained at Sanctuary for about a week training the outpost's tavern-keeper, Tracy. It was a week full of extravagant meals and a seemingly bottomless tankard of grog. Soon pirates near and far heard the tale of Chef Hendrick's quest and began chasing him from outpost to outpost.

I too took to the seas in tow, to see and taste for myself what delicacies each tavern-keeper was bound to create. Of all the Trading Companies that call the Sea of Thieves home, The Hunter's Call holds a special place in my heart–well, my stomach really. With their plunder of fresh ingredients, my black-market connections and the Merchant Alliance at every outpost, each tavern-keeper has been able to create their own menus and specialties. Now I simply walk into any tavern, grab a seat, and shout "Go on, surprise me!"

THE TAVERNS

From the sandy beaches and turquoise waters that are the Shores of Plenty to the fiery molten hellscapes that dot the Devil's Roar, each region in the Sea of Thieves has its own atmosphere, its own spirit and terrain based on the sea's topography, and of course its own unique taverns. Each tavern-keeper has access to regional fish and plenty of bananas, coconuts, pomegranates, mangoes, and pineapples to load up the supply barrels.

Tavern chefs also have access to the islands' bounty of wildlife like chickens, pigs, and snakes to butcher into tantalizing main plates. Dangerous sharks and Megalodons roam the waves, and are more plentiful here in the Sea of Thieves than in the wider world, so tavern-keepers take utmost care when considering adding them to their menus. Even the elusive Kraken is fair game as they can be truly tender and delectable when prepared by a master!

This journal takes you on my culinary quest throughout the Sea of Thieves as I sailed along Chef Hendrick's route, to every tavern, recording all the new and exciting meals I sampled. What he leaves behind at each outpost is a revival of the pirating spirit, something new, exciting, and uncharted. I've always been one to set course for new islands and new paths, and this was indeed a new and delicious voyage with undiscovered riches.

THE SHORES OF PLENTY

Is this your first visit to the Shores of Plenty?
Well then, my pirate friend, you are surely in for a treat.

With its crystal blue waters, bright sunny skies, and pristine beaches, this tropical region is gorgeous to be sure, and a delight for any buccaneer willing to take on pirating adventures while gazing at golden sunsets. The Merchant Alliance is always looking to trade and, of course, this means there are always fresh supplies to be had. The Shores are also home to two outposts and taverns which have some of the region's freshest and most delectable dishes inspired by the sea's abundance of Plentifins and the islands' bountiful source of bananas and coconuts.

The George and Kraken is the tavern at Sanctuary Outpost, and is run by a tavern-keeper named Tracy, who comes from a long line of tavern-keepers and pours some tasty grog. Sanctuary also happens to be where I myself first landed as a stowaway and set up my own stall selling bananas to fund my pirating adventures. Over on Port Merrick, it's Tina who runs things at **The Captains' Head** tavern, where I hear she makes a house chili that is legendary. If your ship's barrels are full of bananas, coconuts, and bait then you are ready for a feast sure to impress even the Pirate Lord himself. Grab a storage crate, collect your ingredients, head to your ship's galley, and start the Shores of Plenty recipes.

Culinary adventure calls!

MERCHANT ALLIANCE SUPPLY CRATE BASICS

Making sure you have the basics in the galley for any journey across the seas is the Merchant Alliance's goal. These are the staples needed for many of the dishes prepared by the talented tavern-keepers. I will say, pickled onions do smell and taste better when you're not hiding in a barrel of them.

Pickled Onions

1. Slice the onion into thin rings and put into a lidded jar (with around 3 cups capacity). In a small pot bring ½ cup water to a soft boil and immediately remove from the heat. Add the sugar and stir until dissolved.

2. Return to the heat and mix in the vinegar, juices, salt, oregano, coriander seeds, and peppercorns. Warm, but do not allow to boil, for 2 minutes and remove from the heat. Pour the warm liquid over the onions in the jar and give it a good stir.

3. Allow to cool uncovered for about 30 minutes. Close the jar and leave to marinate in the fridge for at least two hours, best overnight. You can use the liquid for Pomegranate Dressing (see page 12) and Jicama Slaw (see page 38).

INGREDIENTS

- 1 very large white or red onion, thinly sliced
- 1 tbsp sugar
- 1 cup white vinegar
- ¼ cup lime juice
- ¼ cup mango juice
- 1 tsp salt
- 1 tsp dried oregano
- 1 tsp coriander seeds
- 1 tsp black peppercorns

 Easy **Prep:** 10 minutes **Inactive:** 2.5 hrs **Active:** 10 minutes 1 quart Vegan

INGREDIENTS

- 2 cups mango juice
- 1 tsp ground ginger
- 4 tsp curry powder
- 2 tbsp lime juice
- 2 tbsp agave syrup
- 2 tbsp rice wine vinegar
- ¼ tsp salt

Curried Mango Sauce

1. In medium saucepan over low to medium heat whisk together the mango juice, ginger, curry powder, lime juice, and agave syrup. Whisking every 2 minutes or so, cook and reduce by half until thickened–about 10 minutes.

2. Whisk in the vinegar and salt, then cook for another 2 minutes keeping the sauce thick. Serve with Magpie's Wings (see page 22).

 Easy  **Prep:** 2 minutes **Active:** 15 minutes 1 pint Vegan

Pineapple Orange Dipping Sauce

1. In a small bowl, whisk together 1 tbsp water and cornstarch. Set aside. In a medium saucepan, mix ¾ cup water, the crushed pineapple, marmalade, garlic, chilis, sugar, vinegar, and salt. Bring to a boil over medium heat, then reduce the heat and simmer for 5 minutes or until reduced by a third.
2. Whisk the cornstarch mixture and add to sauce, whisking to combine. Cook until thickened (about 3 minutes) and remove from heat. Allow to cool completely and store in the refrigerator in an airtight container. Serve with Coconut Shrimp (see page 20).

INGREDIENTS

- 1 tbsp cornstarch (cornflour)
- ½ cup crushed pineapple
- ¼ cup orange marmalade
- 3 medium cloves garlic, minced
- 2 tsp finely chopped red Thai chilis, seeds removed
- ½ cup sugar
- ½ cup rice vinegar
- 2 tsp salt

 Easy **Prep:** 15 minutes **Active:** 15 minutes 1 pint Vegan

INGREDIENTS

- 1 large egg yolk
- 1 ¼ cup canola (rapeseed) oil
- ½ tsp Dijon mustard
- 1 tbsp rice wine vinegar
- ½ tbsp lemon juice
- Salt

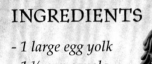

Homemade Mayo

1. In large bowl, add the egg yolk and whisk in 1 tbsp oil until emulsified. Add the mustard and continue whisking. Add the oil 1 tbsp at a time, making sure the oil is completely combined into the emulsification and the mayo is thick. Continue until you have added ½ cup oil and then add a splash each of water, vinegar, and lemon juice.
2. Continue whisking in ¼ cup canola oil a little at a time in a continuous drizzle. Continuing with the whisking, add a little bit more water, vinegar, and lemon juice and then drizzle in another ¼ cup oil. Repeat the process until the desired lightness is achieved, then season with salt to taste. Transfer to an airtight container. This mayo will not be as thick as commercially produced mayonnaise.

 Easy **Prep:** 5 minutes **Active:** 10-15 minutes  1 pint Vegetarian

Pomegranate Syrup

1. In large saucepan, mix the pomegranate juice, sugar, and lemon juice. Bring to boil over medium heat, stirring occasionally until reduced to a thick syrup consistency (about 40–45 minutes).
2. Remove from heat and cool slightly, for about 10 minutes. Pour into an airtight bottle.

INGREDIENTS

- 3 cups pomegranate juice
- ¾ cup sugar
- 2 tbsp lemon juice

 Easy  **Active:** 50 minutes 1 cup Vegan

Orange-Infused Olive Oil

1. In a small saucepan, combine the oil and the zest. Bring it to a very light simmer and heat for 3 minutes.
2. Take off the heat, cover the saucepan, and steep until completely cooled. Strain into an airtight bottle.

 Easy **Prep:** 5 minutes **Inactive:** 15 minutes **Active:** 3 minutes 1 cup Vegan

INGREDIENTS

- 1 cup extra virgin olive oil
- Zest from 2 large oranges
- Zest from 1 tangerine

INGREDIENTS

- ¼ cup brown sugar
- ¼ cup tamarind concentrate
- ¾ cup ketchup
- ¼ cup rice wine vinegar
- ¼ cup water
- ½ tbsp Worcestershire sauce
- ½ tbsp dry mustard
- ½ tbsp curry powder
- 1 tsp smoked paprika
- 1 tsp salt
- ½ tsp black pepper
- ½ tsp guajillo chili powder

Pendragon's BBQ Sauce

1. Add all ingredients to a blender and blend until smooth.
2. Transfer to a 1-pint mason jar. Use to construct Pendragon's BBQ Chicken Pizza (see page 104).

 Easy **Prep:** 5 minutes **Active:** 5 minutes 1 pint Vegan

Pomegranate Dressing

1. In a medium bowl, whisk all ingredients except the oil. Whisk in the oil slowly until emulsified.
2. Transfer to a sealable dressing jar. When ready to serve, shake and drizzle.

 Easy 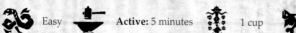 **Active:** 5 minutes 1 cup Vegan

INGREDIENTS

- 3 tbsp pomegranate syrup
- 2 tbsp white wine vinegar
- 1 tsp Dijon mustard
- 2 tbsp lime juice
- 4 tbsp pickled onion brine (see Pickled Onions page 10)
- Salt and pepper
- 5 tbsp canola (rapeseed) oil

THE GEORGE AND KRAKEN

Sanctuary Outpost is a bright, welcoming island located in the northwest region of the Shores of Plenty. It consists of four islands, with The George and Kraken tavern on the main shore backing into a large rock formation. This is where Tracy has been serving the "greasiest grog" since the day she could reach the tap on the grog barrel. She comes from a family of tavern-keepers, with her own great-great-grandmother opening the very first tavern, "Travelers' Rest." Nights here are lively to be sure,

but any time can be an exciting time at the GNK, with the liveliest of events being the Old Age Pirates' lunch. Well, it's more of a Pirate's "Punch"–after a few grogs there are always plenty of gold teeth lying about.

I had my first grog here when I arrived in the Sea of Thieves, and my first meal. Since then, the grub has gotten much better. I've heard that Shipwright Sherry's favorite is Magpie's Wings, she just loves rhyming it with things. Overheard on the dock, Chief Trader Mollie speaks very highly of the coconut cake, although I think she prefers Tina's House Chili over at The Captain's Head–it doesn't have any animals in it.

If you find yourself anchored at Sanctuary, don't forget to treat your crew to a grog, a meal, and a song before you sail along.

KRAKEN INK PASTA WITH SHRIMP

While it's fun to go hunt down your own Kraken and harvest the ink yourself for this umami-filled dish, I would highly recommend stopping by the Merchant Alliance and chatting with Mavis. She is sure to have some Kraken Ink Pasta in one of her storage crates. If you're having trouble finding a Kraken, you could always substitute squid!

 Easy

 Prep: 15 minutes
Inactive: 8.5 hours
Active: 20 minutes

 Serves 2

 Pescatarian

1. This recipe is usually started in the morning before most pirates set sail for the day. Skin the entire garlic head and add to a food processor. Add the olive oil, sea salt, and juice from ½ lemon and process until smooth. Add the mixture to a large resealable plastic bag or sealable glass container, along with the shrimp. Marinate in the refrigerator for 8–24 hours.

2. When ready to cook, remove from the refrigerator and allow to come to room temperature for 30 minutes. Fill ¾ of a large pot with water and 1 tbsp kosher salt. Bring to a boil. Add the pasta, cook to desired doneness, and drain.

3. While the pasta is cooking, in a large skillet over low heat melt the butter and add the shrimp with all the marinade. Cook on low for 5 minutes, then increase heat to medium, add pepper flakes, juice from the other lemon half, and cook for another few minutes or until the shrimp are fully opaque. Add the Parmesan. Transfer the pasta to a shrimp skillet and with tongs carefully flip to coat all the pasta with the sauce. Serve with parsley, more Parmesan, and cracked, and enjoy while envisioning your next Kraken Hunter commendation.

INGREDIENTS

- 1 head of garlic
- ¼ cup olive oil
- 1 tsp sea salt
- 1 lemon
- 1 lb raw large 21/30-size shrimp, shelled and deveined
- 1 tbsp kosher salt (flaky sea salt)
- 1 lb Kraken (squid) ink pasta, such as fettucine
- ¼ cup butter
- ½ cup grated Parmesan cheese, plus more for serving
- ¼ tsp pepper flakes
- 1 tbsp chopped parsley
- Cracked pepper

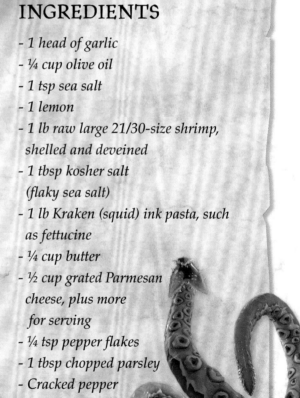

THE GEORGE AND KRAKEN CHICKEN SANDWICH

It's a wonderful sight to see, stacks of chicken coops on the dock. A tell-tale sign the tavern will be a bevy of activity very soon. For it is hard to resist the savory aroma of the tavern's signature sandwich as it delightfully draws pirates in for a tasty meal, much like those rashers did for me on my first day.

 Easy

 Prep: 1.5 hours **Active:** 10 minutes

 Serves 4

Pickled Carrots

1. Add the carrots to an airtight glass pickling container.
2. Add the remaining ingredients to a small pan and bring to a light boil to dissolve the sugar and salt. Pour over the carrots. Allow to cool slightly, cover, and refrigerate.

For the sandwiches

1. Pound the chicken breasts in between plastic wrap to ¼-inch-thick slices. Cut it into 2 equal pieces. Add salt and pepper to taste and set aside.
2. Add the cumin, garlic, salt, and pepper to the panko crumbs. Whisk the eggs and Worcestershire sauce in separate bowl.

In shallow plates or bowls, prepare 3 dredging stations: 1. Flour and cornstarch 2. Egg mixture 3. Panko mixture. Dredge the cutlets 1 at a time, starting with the flour mixture, then the egg mixture, and finally the panko mixture. Set aside.

3. Heat the oil in pan to 360°F, then fry the breaded cutlets on each side for 2–3 minutes until golden. Remove from oil and drain on paper towels.
4. To serve, heat up a large flat skillet or griddle, split the rolls in half lengthwise, butter each side and toast lightly. Build the sandwich with lettuce, tomato, pickled carrot, and chicken cutlet, then top with 1 tbsp Ancients' Dressing and cilantro.

INGREDIENTS

- 2 chicken breasts, making 4 cutlets
- ½ tsp cumin
- ½ tsp garlic powder
- ½ tsp salt
- Freshly ground pepper
- 1 ½ cups panko crumbs
- 2 large eggs
- 1 tsp Worcestershire sauce
- 1 cup all-purpose (plain) flour
- 1 tbsp cornstarch (cornflour)
- 2 cups vegetable oil

For the sandwiches
- 4 Portuguese rolls or bolillos
- 2 tbsp butter
- Lettuce
- Tomato
- Pickled Carrots
- Cilantro (coriander)
- Ancients' Dressing (see page 40)
- Pickled Onions (see page 10) (optional)

Pickled Carrots
- 6 carrots, sliced into ribbons
- ½ cup white rice wine vinegar
- 1 cup coconut water
- ¼ cup sugar
- ½ tsp kosher salt (flaky sea salt)
- ½ tsp coriander seeds

COCONUT SHRIMP

Ocean Crawlers are no match for the culinary imagination at Sanctuary Outpost. I swear Tracy can do almost anything with a coconut and a little fire. Careful, these pack a little heat. I think she serves these just to sell more grog.

 Easy

 Prep: 20 minutes
Active: 15–30 minutes

 Serves 4

 Spicy

1. Season the shrimp with the salt on both sides and set aside. Set up the dredging station. In a medium bowl, whisk the eggs and soy sauce and set aside. In another medium bowl, combine the breadcrumbs and both coconut flakes. In another medium bowl, mix the flour, cornstarch, chipotle powder, and granulated garlic and set it aside.

2. In a deep pan or pot, heat the oil to 350°F. Using different pairs of tongs for this process, and dredging 3 shrimp at a time, coat the shrimp in the flour cornstarch mixture on both sides, then drop them into the egg mixture. Using another pair of tongs, remove the shrimp from the egg mixture, drop and coat them on both sides with the coconut mixture. Place them on a paper towel laid on a plate.

3. Using another set of tongs, place 3 shrimp at a time in the oil, and fry for 2–3 minutes until golden brown. Be careful not to overcrowd and keep a watchful eye on the temperature–keep it within 340–360°F as best you can. Use a spider strainer to remove them and place on paper towels to drain. Serve with Pineapple Orange Dipping Sauce (see page 11), Captain Briggsy's Black Beans and Plantains (see page 74), and Pineapple Rice (see page 108).

INGREDIENTS

- 1 lb raw 16/20-size shrimp, peeled and deveined
- 1 tsp sea salt
- 2 large eggs
- 1 tbsp low-sodium soy sauce
- ½ cup panko breadcrumbs
- 1 cup sweetened coconut flakes
- 1 cup unsweetened coconut flakes
- ¼ cup all-purpose (plain) flour
- 2 tbsp cornstarch (cornflour)
- 1 tsp chipotle powder
- 1 tsp granulated garlic
- 3 cups canola (rapeseed) oil for frying

MAGPIE'S WINGS

Named after the first ship to sail the Sea of Thieves, the Pirate Lord himself was known to enjoy a few dozen of these double-cooked, extra-crispy wings. Make sure to dip your hands in the water after enjoying a plate or two, otherwise your sail-hoisting duties may be a little sticky.

 Moderate

 Prep: 10 minutes
Inactive: 2 hours
Active: 25–40 minutes

 Serves 3

1. Heat the oil in large Dutch oven to 250°F. Do not split wings. Cook all wings for 20–25 minutes or until tender but not browned. Remove from the oil, transfer to a rack on a baking sheet lined with paper towel, and let stand for 2 hours.

2. When oil cools, pour it though a filter to re-use. Clean out the Dutch oven so you don't burn anything left in the pot. The wings at this point can be refrigerated or even frozen.

3. When ready to serve, in small saucepan melt the butter and add garlic through a garlic press. Reduce the heat to low and continue to slowly cook the garlic butter mixture for another 2 minutes, taking care not to burn the butter or garlic. Add the lime juice and cilantro and set aside.

4. Heat the oil to 400°F and add the chicken wings in batches, taking care not to overcrowd. Cook until golden brown and crisp, 3–5 minutes, or to your preferred level of crispness. Transfer to a wire rack and salt immediately, then place in large bowl and coat with the garlic butter. Serve with Curried Mango Sauce (see page 10).

INGREDIENTS

- 6 cups canola (rapeseed) oil
- 3 lbs chicken wings
- 2 tbsp butter
- 2 cloves garlic
- Juice from half a lime
- 1 tbsp chopped cilantro (coriander) leaves
- Salt

MARAUDER'S MASH

Leaving them with that warm feeling they only get when trading in a galleon-full of treasure chests, this comfort dish is so rich that it has become a favorite of marauders near and far.

 Easy   **Prep:** 25 minutes **Active:** 40 minutes   Serves 6

1. Wash, peel, and cut the potatoes into quarters. Fill a large stock pot ¾ of the way with water and add 1 tbsp salt. Add the potatoes, bring to a boil, and cook for 20 minutes or until they are fork tender.

2. Using a slotted spoon, remove the potatoes and add to a potato ricer a few at a time. Press into large mixing bowl. Add the chicken stock and cream and mix thoroughly. Melt the clarified butter in microwave or in small pan over low heat. Add to the potatoes and blend until silky smooth. Taste for seasoning. Transfer to serving bowl and top with butter.

INGREDIENTS

- 2 lbs Yukon Gold or Butter Potatoes
- 1 tbsp kosher salt (flaky sea salt), plus more for seasoning
- ¼ cup chicken stock
- ¾ cup cream
- ½ cup clarified butter
- 2 tbsp unsalted butter

COCONUT RICE

At Sanctuary Outpost coconut rice is a staple side dish. But I've heard that the Merchant Alliance has begun trading it as a commodity with other outposts. Seems Tina over at The Captain's Head claims it pairs perfectly with her legendary Chili. I might have to sloop it over there and try it.

 Easy   **Prep:** 25 minutes **Active:** 30 minutes   Serves 4   Vegan

1. Put the rice in a heat-proof bowl and add boiling water. Cover and allow to stand for 20 minutes.

2. In medium pan over medium heat, melt the coconut oil and butter. Add the onion and sauté till soft.

3. Drain the rice through a mesh strainer to remove as much water as possible, then add to the onion mixture and fry the rice until a nutty color. Add the vegetable stock, coconut milk, granulated garlic, and salt, and mix. Bring to a boil, reduce heat to simmer and cover. Cook for 15 minutes–do not uncover. After 15 minutes remove from heat and allow to stand for 15 minutes. Uncover and fluff.

INGREDIENTS

- 1 cup long grain rice
- 1 tbsp coconut oil
- 1 tbsp vegetable butter
- ½ medium white onion, chopped
- 1 cup unsalted vegetable stock
- 1 cup coconut milk
- ½ tsp granulated garlic
- 1 tsp sea salt

COCONUT CAKE

I swear Tracy pillaged every barrel on this island for every last coconut to make this cake. I asked, and Tracy claims she created this cake for those pirates who need some extra calm seas and a sweet treat as they set sail.

 Complex

 Prep: 30 minutes
Inactive: 3 hours
Active: 30 minutes

 Serves 8

 Lactose Free

1. Preheat oven to 325°F. Grease and flour two 9-inch round cake pans. All ingredients should be at room temperature. Sift the flour into a large bowl. Whisk the baking soda, baking powder, and salt into the flour until totally incorporated. In a stand mixer bowl using an electric hand mixer, cream the butter and sugar together for 3 minutes until creamy. Add the eggs one at a time, making sure to fully incorporate them before adding the next one. Add the yogurt, sour cream, and both extracts.

2. Secure the bowl to the stand mixer and using a paddle attachment, mix in half the dry ingredients and half the coconut milk. Mix until incorporated, using a spatula to scrape down the bowl, and add the other half of flour and coconut milk. Set to medium and mix for 2 minutes or until fully incorporated. Remove the bowl and fold in the coconut flakes.

3. Pour equal portions into the 2 cake pans. Bake for 30–35 minutes or until a cake tester comes out clean. Transfer to cooling racks. Remove the cakes from cake pans after 15 minutes and continue to cool for another 2 hours.

4. For the frosting, in the stand mixer add 1 cup of plant butter and 2 cups of powdered sugar and mix until incorporated. Add the rest of the butter and sugar and continue to mix until fully incorporated. Add the milks and extracts. Mix on medium speed for 3 minutes until creamy. Frost the cake and top with toasted coconut.

INGREDIENTS

Cake
- 2 ½ cups cake (plain) flour
- ½ tsp baking soda
- 2 tsp baking powder
- 1 tsp salt
- 1 cup vegetable butter
- 1 cup sugar
- 4 large eggs
- ½ cup vanilla coconut yogurt
- 3 tbsp lactose free sour cream
- 2 tsp coconut extract
- 1 tsp vanilla extract
- 1 ¼ cup coconut milk
- 1 cup sweetened coconut flakes

Frosting
- 1 ½ cups vegetable butter
- 3 cups powdered (icing) sugar
- 1 tbsp almond milk
- 2 tbsp coconut milk
- 1 tsp vanilla extract
- 1 tbsp coconut extract
- 1 cup coconut flakes, toasted

SEA OF THIEVES GOLD COINS

I like making sure I have at least one last gold piece in my boot for emergencies. It comes in handy, trust me! These coins, however, would leave a few too many crumbs, so it's only right that I finish the whole plate in one sitting (with a nice tankard of coconut milk, of course.)

 Easy   **Prep:** 10 minutes
Inactive: 1–2 hours
Active: 90 minutes   24 cookies   Vegetarian

1. Whisk the flour, baking soda, baking powder, and sea salt together in a small bowl. Cream the sugars, butter, and coconut oil together in a large bowl with an electric hand mixer until smooth. Beat in the egg and extracts and beat for another minute until fully combined. Add enough food coloring to the mixture to get a golden color.
2. Blend in a third of the flour mixture, combine, add another third and combine. Add the last third and combine with a spatula or your hands, wearing food-safe gloves.

3. Roll out on lightly floured surface, knead, and form into two dough balls. Roll them onto parchment paper to desired thickness–¼ inch is good. Place the parchment on a cookie sheet and cut rounds using a cookie cutter. Remove scraps and on floured surface continue to roll out, cut rounds and transfer to parchment on cookie sheet until you have 12 cookie rounds per cookie sheet.
4. If you are using a cookie stamp, refrigerate for one hour before stamping the cookies. Preheat the oven to 375°F. Bake until edges are golden, 8–10 minutes. Remove from oven and let sit for two minutes before transferring to a wire rack to cool completely.
5. Make the frosting by combining all ingredients. Use yellow and a touch of red to make a "gold" frosting and use a piping bag with a small-diameter tip to frost the cookie coins. Let dry completely before eating, roughly 1 hour.

INGREDIENTS

Coins
- 2 ½ cups all-purpose (plain) flour
- ½ tsp baking soda
- 1 tsp baking powder
- ½ tsp sea salt
- 1 ¼ cup powdered sugar
- ¼ cup coconut palm sugar
- ½ cup vegetable butter, softened
- ½ cup coconut oil, solid
- 1 large egg
- ½ tsp vanilla extract
- ½ tsp coconut extract
- Gold food coloring

Sovereign Frosting
- 3 cups powdered sugar
- 4–6 tbsp coconut milk
- 2 tsp meringue powder
- ¼ tsp coconut extract
- Red and yellow food coloring

Special equipment: cookie stamp, piping bags, and tips

SUNSET OVER CRESCENT ISLE

Ahh, this refreshing drink soothes a sailor's soul.

1. Fill a tall glass with ice. Add all the juices to a drink mixer, with ice. Shake and strain into the glass and top off with ginger beer.
2. Slowly drizzle the grenadine over the top. Enjoy while watching the sun slowly fade into the turquoise waters. Add rum if of pirate drinking age.

INGREDIENTS

- 1 oz lime juice
- 1 oz pineapple juice
- 1 oz mango juice
- 4 oz ginger beer
- ½ oz grenadine

SEA OF THIEVES GROG

The original and still the best in my opinion.
Tracy pulls the best Grog in the Shores!

1. In a drink mixer combine the sugar and lime juice until the sugar dissolves. Add ice cubes, rum, and coconut water.
2. Shake well until fully blended. Pour into a glass or tankard with or without ice. Garnish with lime to prevent scurvy.

INGREDIENTS

- 3 tsp coconut palm sugar
- 1 oz fresh lime juice
- 1 oz good dark rum
- 4 oz coconut water
- Limes

THE CAPTAIN'S HEAD

Port Merrick consists of a newly renovated fortified town with shops and newly constructed wharfs, Trading Company buildings, and even a lighthouse. At the town center is The Captain's Head, formerly a tavern, now a bustling inn. Tina is the tavern-keeper here and is the life of the party. The new upgrades to the outpost and to the tavern have freed Tina up to really get creative with her menu. As part of the Shores of Plenty she of course uses ingredients like bananas and coconuts to create masterpieces. She not only has a signature drink, Captain's Punch, but she also has a recipe for meatless chili that is legendary. Chief Trader Mollie swears by it!

Chef Hendrick spent a little more time here than at most outposts as the islets and bridges got a little confusing after a night of training and grogging. Which is lucky for all who anchor up at Port Merrick. Sharon the shipwright swears "YOU HAVE TO TRY THE PLENTIFIN TACOS!" And when it comes to desserts, Madame Olga is a big fan of Smoked Banana Bread Pudding, I think mostly because it has smoke.

This is the southernmost tavern within the Shores of Plenty and is a perfect launching point for adventure. Just don't party too much with Tina and forget to load up on supplies before you set sail.

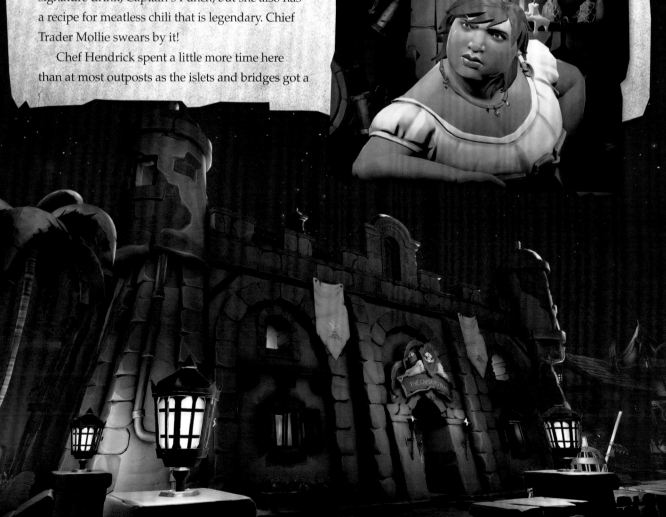

TINA'S HOUSE CHILI

On the way back to the outpost some of our swashbuckling buccaneers harpooned a few crates full of exotic spices and rather than turn them in for gold, they donated them to the tavern so that we could make Tina's delicious, legendary chili. Hold the meat!

 Moderate   **Prep:** 30 minutes **Active:** 1 hour   Serves 6   Vegan

1. In dry pan, toast the guajillo pepper strips lightly until fragrant. Place in bowl and cover with hot water until reconstituted. Reserve the liquid.

2. In a Dutch oven, heat the oil and add the onion and 1 tsp of salt and cook till translucent. Add the garlic and cook another minute. Add the tomato paste and spices and cook for another minute. Stir in the potatoes, yam, tomato sauce, 1 tsp salt and 3 cups of water. Bring to a boil, then reduce heat to medium-low and simmer until the potatoes are tender, about 30 minutes. Allow to cool slightly.

3. Add one cup potatoes and one cup of cooking liquid with the guajillo pepper to a blender and puree until thick and smooth. Add the reserved guajillo water if the puree is too thick. Return to the Dutch oven and add the last tsp salt and the cannellini beans. Bring to a boil over high heat, then reduce to medium and cook for 10 minutes. Taste for seasoning and serve with avocado, limes, and coconut rice–or whatever crispy cracker the tavern-keeper has on hand.

INGREDIENTS

- 2 dried guajillo peppers, de-seeded and sliced into strips
- 2 tbsp coconut oil
- ½ medium white onion, chopped
- 3 tsp kosher salt (flaky sea salt)
- 4 cloves garlic, minced
- 2 tbsp tomato paste
- 2 tsp chili powder
- 1 tsp ground cardamon
- 1 tsp ground cumin
- 1 tsp ground coriander
- ½ tsp cinnamon
- ½ tsp ground ginger
- ½ tsp Turkish sumac
- 2 cups peeled, chopped Japanese sweet potatoes
- 2 cups peeled, chopped Yukon gold potato
- 1 cup peeled, chopped yam
- 1 cup tomato sauce
- 1 x 15-oz can cannellini beans, drained and rinsed
- Avocado
- Limes

THE PORT MERRICK BREAKFAST

While I remember my first breakfast at Sanctuary Outpost fondly, I must admit that bananas do have a special hold on me. They were once my only source of gold after all, and the breakfast here at The Captain's Head, well, it's all about the bananas.

Golden Smoothie

1. Trim off the banana ends and using a sharp knife or dagger cut down one of the seams of the bananas. Carefully remove the peels and set aside for Golden Bacon.
2. Add the bananas to the blender with all the other ingredients and set on liquify. Blend until smooth and enjoy while equipping your Sloop for a voyage.

 Easy   **Prep:** 2 minutes **Active:** 1 minute Serves 2 Vegan

INGREDIENTS

- 2 very ripe bananas
- 1 tbsp agave syrup
- 1 cup frozen mango chunks
- 2 cups coconut milk
- 1 tsp vanilla extract

INGREDIENTS

- 2 very ripe banana peels from the Golden Smoothie
- 2 tbsp soy sauce
- 1 tbsp mirin
- 1 tsp coconut aminos
- ½ tsp liquid smoke
- 1 tbsp agave syrup
- ½ tsp smoked paprika
- ½ tsp garlic powder
- 2 tbsp coconut oil

Golden Bacon

1. After you cut up the bananas for your smoothie now it's time to make the bacon! Cut the peels into 4 strips per banana. Place the peels on cutting board and using the back of a butter knife scrape off the inside of the banana peel until it is almost translucent. In a small bowl mix all the ingredients together except the oil. Add the peels to a large resealable plastic bag and add the marinade to cover. Marinate for one hour.
2. Heat the coconut oil in a cast iron pan over medium heat. Remove the banana peels from the marinade and drain any excess liquid. Add the peels to the pan and fry each side for 1 minute, until golden brown. Remove from pan and drain on paper towel. Enjoy!

 Easy **Prep:** 5 minutes **Inactive:** 1 hour **Active:** 3 minutes Serves 2 Vegan

PLENTIFIN FISH TACOS

The best part of the Shores of Plenty are the Plentifins. They are fresh, tasty, and considered good luck. Building your own Plentifin Tacos at The Captain's Head is very rewarding, there is no right or wrong way. It's much like how you prepare to sail–pirate's choice!

 Easy

 Prep: 1 hour
Inactive: 1 hour
Active: 30 minutes

 Serves 6

 Pescatarian

1. Heat the oil in deep pan over medium-high heat to get to 350°F. Slice the fillets into strips, about 6 per fillet. Salt the fish lightly with 1 tsp salt.

2. Combine all other dry ingredients and 1 tsp salt in mixing bowl and whisk in seltzer until all lumps are gone and the batter has a smooth consistency. Dip the fish in the batter and then place in oil. Deep fry for 5–7 minutes, continuing to flip, until golden brown and crispy on all sides. Set aside on paper towels to drain.

Jicama Slaw

1. Combine all the prepared veggies in large bowl with salt and toss well. Set aside.

2. Whisk together all other ingredients until completely combined. Dress the slaw with the mixture, toss until coated, cover, and refrigerate for at least one hour.

Chipotle Crema

1. Combine all ingredients in a blender and process till smooth. Refrigerate.

INGREDIENTS

- 3 cups canola (rapeseed) oil
- 3 tilapia fillets
- 2 tsp salt
- 1 cup flour
- ¼ tsp garlic powder
- ¼ tsp ancho chili powder
- ½ tsp baking powder
- 1 cup seltzer water
- 1 tbsp toasted unsweetened coconut
- Flour tortillas

Chipotle Crema

- 1 cup Mexican crema or sour cream
- 1 large chipotle pepper in adobo sauce
- 1 tbsp lime juice
- ¼ tsp salt

Jicama Slaw

- ½ cup carrots, finely julienned
- ½ cup red cabbage, shredded
- 1 cup green cabbage, shredded
- 2 cups jicama, finely julienned
- ¼ cup red onion, sliced
- ¼ cup cilantro (coriander), chopped
- ½ tsp salt
- 6 tbsp Pickled Onion brine (see page 10)
- 3 tbsp lime juice
- 4 tbsp olive oil
- 2 tbsp agave syrup
- ½ tsp each: cumin, ancho chili, and garlic powder
- ½ tsp oregano

HEARTS OF PALM SALAD WITH ANCIENTS' DRESSING

The Ancients have many secrets and while their legendary voyages are treacherous and challenging, they can also inspire. With its glowing green phantoms, green tornado, and emerald stones, the Legend of the Veil was the muse for this salad and dressing.

 Easy   **Prep:** 12 minutes **Active:** 6 minutes   Serves 4   Vegetarian

1. Place all the dressing ingredients except the the oil in a food processor or blender and process until smooth. Add the oil and process. Taste and season and blend until preferred consistency is attained. Add more oil if necessary.

2. Drain and rinse the hearts of palm in cold water. Cover with cold water and set aside. Chop up the carrots, cucumber, and onions. Toss the romaine and arugula with all the veggies, season with kosher salt and pepper, and top with sliced hearts of palm. Finish with the dressing and give it a quick toss.

INGREDIENTS

Dressing
- 2 cups Homemade Mayo (see page 11)
- 2 cups parsley
- 1 cup mixed fresh herbs: dill, mint, and cilantro (coriander)
- 4 tbsp chopped chives
- 2 tbsp lemon juice
- 1 tsp lime zest
- 1 tsp coconut aminos
- 2 garlic cloves minced
- ½ tsp kosher salt (flaky sea salt)
- freshly ground pepper
- 4 tbsp extra virgin olive oil

Salad
- 1 x 15-oz can hearts of palm
- 1 cup heirloom carrots, varying colors
- 1 cup English cucumber
- ¼ cup green (spring) onions
- 2 cups romaine
- 2 cups arugula (rocket)
- 1 tsp kosher salt (flaky sea salt)
- freshly ground black pepper

BANANA COCONUT CREAM PIE

Banana. Coconut. Cream. Pie. That is all.

 Moderate

 Prep: 30 minutes
Inactive: 9 hours
Active: 1 hour

 Serves 8

 Vegetarian

Crust

1. In large bowl, combine the flour and salt. Mix in the butter with a fork or your hands until coarse. In a small bowl beat the egg yolk with a whisk and add to the flour mix. Add the toasted coconut, then add the seltzer water 1 tbsp at a time and mix until the dough comes together into a ball. Flatten into a disk and wrap in plastic wrap. Refrigerate for 30 minutes.

2. When ready to use, dust flour on a working surface and roll out dough to fit a 9-inch cast iron pan. Preheat the oven to 425° F. Spray the pan with nonstick cooking spray. Carefully press the dough into pan, and using a fork puncture a few holes into the bottom and sides of the pie crust. Cut some parchment paper a little larger than the pan, place it on the pie crust and add pie weights. Blind bake the pie crust for 15 minutes or until golden brown. Remove and allow to cool completely. Refrigerate.

Filling

1. In a small bowl, whisk together the cream and coconut milk to make half and half and set aside. In a large bowl, whisk together the egg yolks, coconut palm sugar, yuzu starch, salt, and flour. Add in 1 cup half and half.

2. In a medium saucepan, over medium heat, combine 1 cup half and half, 1 cup coconut cream, and ½ cup sugar and bring almost to a boil. Remove from heat and, using a measuring cup, add a little of the milk mixture to the beaten eggs while whisking to temper the eggs. Add slowly and continue whisking until 1 cup of the milk mixture has been mixed with the eggs. Pour the egg mixture into the saucepan with the milk mixture and, over a low heat, whisk until it becomes thick. Remove from the heat, and add the extracts and coconut, stirring until evenly combined. Transfer to large bowl and cover the surface with plastic wrap to avoid a skin. Refrigerate for 4 hours.

3. Slice 1 banana and layer it on the base of the crust. Slice the other banana and fold it into the filling. Pour the chilled filling over the bananas and crust. Refrigerate for another 4 hours.

Topping

1. In a large bowl using an electric mixer with a whisk attachment, whip the cream, sugar, and extracts until stiff. Remove the pie from refrigerator. Spread the whipped cream over the top and sprinkle with toasted coconut.

INGREDIENTS

Pie Crust
- 1 cup all-purpose (plain) flour
- ¼ tsp salt
- ½ cup cold butter, cut into small pieces
- 1 egg yolk
- ½ cup sweetened coconut, toasted and cooled
- 3 tbsp cold seltzer (sparkling) water

Filling

- 1 cup heavy (double) cream
- 1 cup coconut milk
- 4 large egg yolks
- ¼ cup coconut palm sugar
- 3 tbsp yuzu starch
- ¼ tsp salt
- ⅓ cup all-purpose flour
- 1 cup coconut cream
- ½ cup sugar
- 1 tsp each vanilla and coconut extract
- 1 ½ cups sweetened coconut
- 2 bananas

Topping

- 2 cups heavy (double) cream
- 2 tbsp powdered (icing) sugar
- 1 tsp coconut extract
- 1 tsp vanilla extract
- 1 cup sweetened shredded coconut

BANANA BREAD

Banana bread is just one of the many tasty treats one can make with bananas. Here at The Captain's Head they add coconut to it and they even bake an extra loaf for a special dessert they cook with smoke. It's quite delicious and not something a skelly can be seen pulling out of thin air.

 Easy

 Prep: 15 minutes
Active: 1 hour

 1 loaf

 Vegetarian

1. Set an oven rack to the middle position and preheat the oven to 350°F. Butter a 9 × 5-inch loaf pan. In a large bowl, whisk the flour, baking soda, salt, cinnamon, and ginger together.

2. Using a stand mixer fitted with a paddle attachment, beat the butter and coconut palm sugar together on high speed until creamy and fluffy, about 2 minutes. Drop the speed to medium and add the eggs one at a time, beating well until fully incorporated. Add the yogurt, mashed bananas, and vanilla extract on medium speed until combined.

3. On low, slowly beat the dry ingredients into the wet ingredients until fully incorporated, using a spatula to scrape down the sides of the bowl, and mix once more. Do not overmix. Fold in the coconut. Spoon the batter into the prepared baking pan and bake for 45–55 minutes. Tent the bread with aluminum foil after 30 minutes. Bake until a cake tester or toothpick comes out clean. Remove from the oven, set the pan on a wire rack and allow to cool completely.

SMOKED BANANA BREAD PUDDING

Tina converted a banana barrel into a smoker when Chef Hendrick had his training session here and she has been smoking just about everything imaginable. Remember that extra banana bread I mentioned? Well, Tina smoked it and it is the stuff of legend. It's only found here at Port Merrick and is a pirate favorite.

 Moderate

 Prep: 20 minutes
Inactive: 1.5 hours
Active: 15 minutes

 Serves 8

 Vegetarian

1. Set up your smoker and preheat to 225°F. Add the wood as specified by the manufacturer–pecan or cherry wood is perfect. Arrange the banana bread cubes in a single layer on a small sheet pan or a doubled-up aluminum foil sheet and place in the smoker. Smoke until toasted, 30–45 minutes.

2. Make the custard by placing the cream, milk, sugar, spices, and salt in a heavy saucepan. Bring to a boil over medium heat and whisk to dissolve the sugar. Remove the pan from the heat. Place the eggs, egg yolk, and vanilla extract in a large heatproof bowl and whisk until smooth. Gradually whisk in the hot cream mixture. Add it little by little so as not to curdle the eggs. Add the smoked banana bread and fold until the bread has absorbed most of the custard.

3. Butter a large cast iron skillet and transfer the pudding mixture into it. Dot with banana slices, brown sugar, and butter, pushing the bananas into the pudding with a fork. Increase the smoker heat to 275°F and smoke the pudding until browned on top and the custard is set, 45–60 minutes. (Insert a metal skewer into the center of the pudding–it should come out clean when the custard is set, with an internal temperature of 165°F.) Serve warm with vanilla ice cream or yogurt.

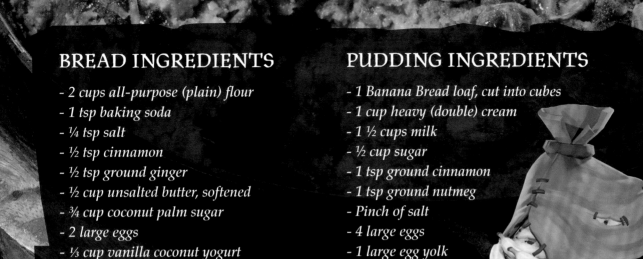

BREAD INGREDIENTS

- 2 cups all-purpose (plain) flour
- 1 tsp baking soda
- ¼ tsp salt
- ½ tsp cinnamon
- ½ tsp ground ginger
- ½ cup unsalted butter, softened
- ¾ cup coconut palm sugar
- 2 large eggs
- ⅓ cup vanilla coconut yogurt
- 2 ⅓ cups (roughly 3 medium bananas) mashed overripe bananas
- 1 tsp vanilla extract
- ¾ cup shredded coconut

PUDDING INGREDIENTS

- 1 Banana Bread loaf, cut into cubes
- 1 cup heavy (double) cream
- 1 ½ cups milk
- ½ cup sugar
- 1 tsp ground cinnamon
- 1 tsp ground nutmeg
- Pinch of salt
- 4 large eggs
- 1 large egg yolk
- 2 tsp vanilla extract
- 1 not yet ripe banana, sliced
- 1 tbsp brown sugar
- 4 tbsp butter, plus extra to grease pan

Special equipment: Smoker

MERCHANT'S FOLLY

1. Add all the ingredients except the blue curacao to a shaker with ice. Shake and then pour over ice cubes in a tumbler.
2. Slowly pour the blue curacao into the middle of the drink. Top with an orange slice and embrace the colors of the Shores of Plenty, for these waters are your passion!

INGREDIENTS

- 1 oz Reposado tequila
- 1 oz coconut rum cream
- ½ oz fresh lime juice
- 4 oz passion fruit juice
- 2 dashes orange bitters
- ½ oz blue curacao
- Orange slice

CAPTAIN'S PUNCH

1. In drink mixer, combine the mint, sugar, and lime juice, and muddle. Add the agave syrup, hibiscus tea, passion fruit juice, and ice cubes.
2. Shake and strain over ice in rocks glasses.

INGREDIENTS

- Mint leaves
- ¼ tsp coconut palm sugar
- 1 oz lime juice
- 1 tsp agave syrup
- 3 oz hibiscus juniper tea (see below)
- 3 oz passion fruit juice

HIBISCUS JUNIPER TEA

1. Crush the juniper berries with a mortar and pestle or with the bottom of a bowl on a cutting board. In small to medium pot, add the hibiscus, crushed berries, and water. Bring to boil, remove from heat, stir, cover, and allow to steep for 1 hour.
2. Add the agave syrup to sealable liquid container and then strain tea through mesh into the container. Allow to cool and refrigerate.

INGREDIENTS

- 2 tbsp juniper berries
- 1 cup dry hibiscus flowers
- 4 cups water
- 3 tbsp agave syrup

THE ANCIENT ISLES

Welcome to the Ancient Isles!

Across this region you will find deep blue waters, glorious waterfalls surrounded by jungle foliage, and ancient ruins. Rock paintings abound here, as do freshwater ponds, intricate caves, and ancient pirate crew hideaways. The islands have an abundance of mango and coconut trees, which heavily influence the cuisine in this region. It's also not uncommon for the chickens, pigs, and snakes that run wild across these islands to find their way into a chef's pan. If fish is on the menu, then it will have to be the indigenous Ancientscale that makes it onto the plate, or the freshwater Pondie, which is also flaky and delectable.

Tanya runs the **Drowned Rat** tavern at Plunder Outpost and serves up one type of grog normally, and she's not one to serve food as it so happens, but with Chef Hendrick's intense training, the food at Plunder is outstanding. It makes sense that the Gold Hoarders frequent the Ancient Isles region— the steak alone here will cost you several gold pieces. Trust me though, it's worth every last coin. Then there's **The Unicorn**, the tavern over at Ancient Spire Outpost that is run by Tasha. She's warm, inviting, and always looking for a little gossip. She cooks up a delectable house roast that is the envy of The Hunter's Call. The Unicorn is also where I have my very own signature dessert. Tasha let me name it for the small price of a juicy tale regarding a certain Pirate Legend, of which I will not say another word. Tasha doesn't like gossips.

THE DROWNED RAT

Plunder Outpost has tall, mountainous, rocky spires, on which the Drowned Rat tavern is the highest building, backing up nicely into the mountain. The tavern-keeper here is Tanya, and she claims to serve only one type of grog: "Chapman's Old Bilge Sniffer." Although to be fair, after Chef Hendrick's visit, the galley at the Rat has been a lot more active. Even though Tanya is not one for frills, she has created a menu that is mouthwatering. She put Eduardo over at the Pirate Emporium to the ultimate test. See, he's always bragging about how he can get anything from the wider world and Tanya finally took him up on his offer. She gave him a scroll full of rare ingredients just to see if he could procure them. Honestly, I think she had a side bet going that he'd come back without a single chest if you ask me.

To Tanya's amazement, Eduardo delivered, and now the Drowned Rat serves Antiquated Coffee Rubbed Steak, which is heavenly. In honor of the Emporium, the tavern has its own Ancient Skelly Rum Drink. It's one that I've even seen Harry the Hoarder leave his tent and shuffle into the tavern for every so often.

No matter how hard Tanya wants to keep her customers hooked on grog only, she makes some truly outstanding meals. Don't leave without trying at least one of them.

ANTIQUATED COFFEE RUB STEAK

While I do have to wait for adventurous pirates to tell me what's on the horizon, I can always smell what's on the menu as taverns prepare meals for famished scallywags. One day I relish and know distinctively is steak day here at Plunder Outpost. After Tasha procures some steaks with some fancy blackmarket trading and secures one of those Siren Shrine antiquated coffee coffers, smoke begins to billow out from the kitchen. Whatever Tanya puts in the rub, it smells and tastes like found treasure!

 Easy

 Prep: 15 minutes
Inactive: 2 hours
Active: 15 minutes

 Serves 2 or 4

1. Prepare butter by bringing it to room temperature and blending it with the coconut oil. Whip it up with a fork so it is all blended. Add 1 tsp salt, the parsley, and chives and mix. Refrigerate to harden.

2. In a small bowl, mix all the other flavorings and coffee to make a steak rub. Place the steaks in a shallow dish and cover with the rub on both sides, then refrigerate for 2 hours. When ready to cook, take the steaks out of the fridge and bring to room temperature. Preheat the oven to 425°F. Preheat a cast iron pan on medium heat and add 1 tbsp of the prepared butter. Place the steak in pan and sear for 4 minutes. Remove from the pan and place raw side down on a meat-safe cutting board, slice, and tent with foil. Keeping the pan on medium heat, bring the pan back up to searing heat, about 1 minute. Add 1 tbsp butter to the pan and the second steak, then repeat the previous steps.

(continued overleaf)

INGREDIENTS

- 3 tbsp butter
- 3 tbsp coconut oil
- 3 tsp kosher salt (flaky sea salt)
- 1 tbsp parsley, finely chopped
- 1 tbsp chives, finely chopped
- 1 tsp chipotle chili powder
- 4 tsp dark brown sugar
- 1 tbsp sweet paprika
- 2 tsp dried oregano
- 1 tsp freshly ground black pepper
- 1½ tsp ground coriander
- 1 tsp onion powder
- 1 tsp ground ginger
- 2 tbsp finely ground coffee beans
- 2 x 16 oz 1-inch thick prime beef steaks

3. Place the sliced steaks, keeping original steak form, into the pan together, raw side down. Cut remaining butter into cubes and dot the steaks with them. Carefully place the pan in the preheated oven and cook for 7 minutes. Remove from the oven and allow to sit for a few minutes, then transfer the steaks to serving plates, and finish with salt flakes.

WHITNEY'S TACOS

The Weaponsmith Whitney came to Plunder and sidled up to the bar asking if there were any meatless tacos on the menu. Well, you can imagine Tanya's response. "No. We don't serve food." So Whitney, being so bighearted and really craving some meatless tacos, offered to cook them on Tuesdays, convincing Tanya that pirates order more grog if they're eating tacos.

 Moderate   **Prep:** 10 minutes **Active:** 15 minutes   Serves 4–6   Vegan

1. In small bowl, whisk together cumin, chili powder, oregano, paprika, cinnamon, and salt, and set aside. Process the jackfruit in a food processor on pulse for a couple of spins until shredded, but no more.

2. Add the coconut oil to a cast iron pan, and over medium heat add the onion and sauté for 2 minutes. Add the garlic and sauté for 1 minute. Add the jackfruit and sauté for another 2 minutes. Add the spice mix, tomato paste, minced chipotle, and liquids, combine and bring to a boil, then reduce to simmer and cook for 5 minutes, stirring occasionally. Turn up the heat and cook for another 5 minutes, stirring and making sure all the liquid is absorbed and the jackfruit gets a little crisp but doesn't stick. Serve on both types of tortillas with cilantro, onion, and a salsa of choice.

INGREDIENTS

- 1 tsp cumin
- 1 tsp guajillo chili powder
- 1 tsp dried oregano
- 1 tsp smoked paprika
- 1 tsp cinnamon
- ½ tsp salt
- 2 x 14 oz cans jackfruit, rinsed and drained
- 2 tbsp coconut oil
- ½ cup red onion, diced
  4 cloves garlic, minced
- 1 tbsp tomato paste

- 1 chipotle pepper in adobo, minced
- ½ cup veggie broth
- ½ cup coconut water
- Corn and flour tortillas
- Cilantro (coriander)
- ¼ cup white onion, finely chopped
- Salsa of choice

 The Ancient Isles

PONDIE FILLETS

Just a short way from here to the east is Devil's Ridge, and a pond teeming with Pondies. They are some of the best fish I've ever had. This recipe stands out for its sweet and spicy profile, as these freshwater fish are marinated in mango juice with just the slightest hint of devilish spice.

 Moderate

 Prep: 5 minutes
Inactive: 15 minutes
Active: 15–20 minutes

 Serves 2

 Pescatarian

1. In a shallow pan, submerge the fillets in mango juice for 15 minutes. In dry pan, toast the coconut and set aside. Heat 1 tbsp oil and 1 tbsp butter together in a skillet over medium heat. Remove the fillets from the mango juice and place them on paper towels to dry them. Add the mango juice to a small saucepan, add the lime juice, 1 tbsp butter, salt, and the chili oil, then simmer to reduce and thicken.

2. Dry the fillets thoroughly and place them skin side down in pan, 2 at a time. Let them cook for 5–7 minutes until the skin is very crisp. Halfway through, tilt the pan towards you and using a large spoon baste the salmon with the juices until fillets are just firm, about 3–5 minutes. Remove from pan, set aside to drain, and tent with foil. Cook the next 2 in the same way. Serve the fillets with the mango sauce. Finish with toasted coconut and finishing salt.

INGREDIENTS

- 4 salmon fillets
- 1 cup mango juice
- 1 tbsp unsweetened shredded coconut
- 2 tbsp coconut oil
- 3 tbsp butter
- 1 tbsp lime juice
- ¼ tsp kosher salt (flaky sea salt)
- 1 tsp chili oil
- Finishing salt

GOLD HOARDERS POTATOES AU GRATIN

The Gold Hoarders help keep business alive in the Ancient Isles, and what better way to show Plunder's appreciation than making a dish lined with gold coins covered in cheese! Well, to be fair it's all potatoes and cheese, but they sure look like crispy, golden, delicious coins.

 Easy   **Prep:** 15 minutes **Active:** 1–1.5 hours   Serves 4   Vegetarian

1. Butter a 10-inch cast iron pan and set aside. Preheat the oven to 400°F. Using a mandolin, slice the potatoes into thin ⅛-inch-coin-size slices and set aside. Add 1 tbsp butter to a fry pan, cook the leeks until soft and translucent, and set aside.

2. In a medium saucepan over medium heat, combine 3 tbsp butter and 3 tbsp flour to make a roux. Whisk till thickened and slightly darkened, slowly whisk in the coconut milk, cream, spices, and the sage, then mix to combine. Heat for another few minutes till heated through. Set aside.

3. Layer a third of the potatoes in a spiral in the buttered pan, layer on some leeks and the cheeses, and add pepper and a little salt. Continue to build layers with the rest of the potatoes, leeks, cheeses, pepper, and salt. Pour the cream mixture over the potatoes. Cover with foil and bake for 1 hour or until just tender when pierced with a knife. Remove foil and continue to bake uncovered for 15 minutes or until cooked through with a crispy top.

PLUNDER CHOP

Pirates sometimes have too much grog, pick up crates on the islands, and feel like chasing a pink- or black-coated pig around. So, from time to time Maureen has some extra pigs that get delivered that have no commission or delivery notes. And that is the short tale of how the Plunder Chop ended up on the menu.

 Easy   **Prep:** 5 minutes **Inactive:** 7 hours **Active:** 15–20 minutes   Serves 2–4

1. In a large pot over high heat, combine all ingredients except the coconut oil and the chops. Bring to a boil, making sure all sugar and salt has been dissolved. Remove from heat and let cool for about two hours, then remove large solids, and add to a large sealable container or plastic bag along with the pork chops. Brine the pork chops for 3–5 hours.

2. Remove and wash off the brine. Dry the pork chops with paper towels. Heat the oil in cast iron pan and sear the chops for 5 minutes on each side. Continue to flip, rendering the fat and getting a nice crust on each side, until the internal temperature is at least 150°F. Remove and let sit for 5 minutes. Serve with Gold Hoarders Potatoes.

POTATOES INGREDIENTS

- 2 lbs russet potatoes, peeled
- 4 tbsp butter
- 1 leek, cleaned and sliced
- 3 tbsp flour
- 1 cup coconut milk
- 1 cup heavy (double) cream
- ⅛ tsp nutmeg
- 1 tsp garlic powder
- 8 fresh sage leaves, finely minced
- ½ cup raclette cheese, shredded
- 1 cup gruyère cheese, shredded
- 1 tsp freshly ground pepper
- 2 tsp salt

CHOP INGREDIENTS

- 6 cups cold water
- ¼ cup apple cider vinegar
- ¼ cup kosher salt
  (flaky sea salt)
- ¼ cup coconut palm sugar
- 1 tbsp black peppercorns
- 1 tbsp dried oregano
- 2 dried bay leaves
- 1 small yellow onion,
  peeled and quartered
- 4 large cloves garlic,
  peeled and smashed
- 2 limes, quartered
- 1 orange, quartered
- 4 thick, bone-in pork chops
- 2 tbsp coconut oil

MANGO SORBET

When Tanya mentioned she wanted to try her luck at making a cold dessert for those hot summer nights, I offered up my mango-cutting skills and helped her create this refreshing treat. Seems all we needed was a couple of barrels, some rock salt she harvested from the sea, some ice she procured from a northern pirate, and convincing her pet monkey to churn it.

 Easy

 Prep: 15 minutes
Inactive: 4 hours
Active: 15 minutes

 2 quarts

 Vegan

1. Add 1 cup water, the sugar, and salt to a saucepan, and heat until fully dissolved to make a simple syrup. Allow to cool completely.
2. Add the mangoes, lime juice, passion fruit juice, and simple syrup to the blender and blend till very smooth and velvety. Transfer to a medium bowl, cover, and refrigerate for 3 hours. Pour into an ice cream maker and follow the manufacturer's directions for sorbet, roughly 40 minutes. Transfer to a container and freeze. Enjoy with a coconut topping.

INGREDIENTS
- *1 cup sugar*
- *⅛ tsp salt*
- *4 cups diced ripe mango*
- *3 tbsp lime juice*
- *1 cup passion fruit juice*
- *sweetened coconut flakes to top*

Special equipment: Ice cream maker

SALTY SEADOG ICE CREAM

This is one of my favorite treats when I visit Plunder Outpost. Its creamy texture reminds me of the buttery sand beach on Cutlass Cay, while the salty caramel hints at the ocean's breeze.

 Easy

 Prep: 10 minutes
Inactive: 3.5 hours
Active: 30 minutes

 Serves 6

 Vegetarian

1. In a heavy medium saucepan, bring the milk and cream to a light boil, remove from flame, and let stand. In a medium bowl, whisk the egg yolks and ¼ cup sugar until pale brown and silky and set aside. In a medium skillet over low heat, add 1 cup sugar and 2 tbsps water and stir until everything is combined and sugar melts and bubbles begin to form, about 3 minutes. Add the butter and combine.

2. Continue to cook, stirring occasionally to make sure the sugar melts evenly, until it is dark amber, thick, and bubbly. Keeping the flame on low, add 1 cup cream and milk mixture to the caramel pan, being extra careful as the mixture will splatter. Continue to cook, stirring until all of caramel has dissolved. Transfer to the milk and cream saucepan, and stir until completely combined. Remove from heat.

3. Add half of the hot milk mixture, ½ cup at a time, in a slow stream, to the eggs, whisking constantly, taking care not to cook the eggs. Pour the egg and milk mixture back into saucepan and cook over medium heat, stirring constantly with a wooden spoon until the temperature reaches 170°F or the custard coats the back of the spoon, roughly 3–5 minutes. Pour the custard through a fine-mesh sieve into a large bowl, then stir in the sea salt and vanilla and allow to cool for 30 minutes. Add plastic wrap to the top of custard to prevent a skin forming. Transfer to refrigerator for 3 hours or overnight.

4. Process in ice cream maker, following the manufacturer's guidelines. Spoon the ice cream into a container, transfer to the freezer, and freeze overnight. Serve with salt flakes and extra caramel if desired.

INGREDIENTS
- 2 cups whole milk
- 2 cups heavy (double) cream
- 3 large egg yolks
- 1 ¼ cups coconut palm sugar
- 4 tbsp unsalted butter
- ½ tsp flaky sea salt
- ½ tsp pure vanilla extract

Special equipment: Ice cream maker

SKINNY PIRATE GROG

Can't fit into your ship's cannon? Skellies outrunning you at every encounter? Sharks seem to be looking at you more intently? It might be time to try Skinny Pirate Grog! This is the perfect choice for the calorie-conscious pirate who can't lay off the grog but needs to shimmy up to the crow's nest a little faster.

Calorie comparisons: Grog: 148 / Skinny Pirate: 88

1. In a drink mixer, combine the sugar substitute and lime juice. Dissolve the sugar.
2. Add ice cubes, rum, and coconut water. Shake well until fully blended. Pour into glass or tankard with or without ice. Garnish with lime.

INGREDIENTS

- 1 oz good dark rum
- 3 tsp brown sugar substitute
- 1 oz fresh lime juice
- 4 oz coconut water
- Ice
- Limes

ANCIENT SKELLY

You hear those clanking, rattling sounds? Quick, look around, hurry, because it can only mean one thing. That Ancient Skelly is ready to drop some Ancient Gold!

1. In a drink mixer, combine all ingredients and shake well, like the jangling of ancient gold coins.
2. Pour into a glass over ice.

INGREDIENTS

- 1 oz rum
- 2 oz banana creme liqueur
- 1 oz lime juice
- 1 oz mango juice
- 1 oz coconut water

THE UNICORN

Ancient Spire Outpost is made up of two islands that are connected by a set of bridges and tunnels, all leading up to The Unicorn tavern at the top of the main island. Not to be missed, if you're in a hurry, are the famed series of ladders leading up to the tavern from behind the Weaponsmith's shop. Tasha is the tavern-keeper here, and she tends to trade in gossip from time to time, although she would never admit to it–she hates gossips. One piece of lore that I know to be true is that the galley fare served up at The Unicorn is top notch. I don't just mean that because it's literally at the top of the island, but because Tasha has become a true master. Take the house roast, for example–Tasha has a hell of a time securing a pig every Sunday from Senior Trader Mildred and climbing that ladder with it, but she does, and with some pineapple and pomegranate turns it into a Pirate Lord-worthy delicacy.

The views here are spectacular, you can see the Devil's Roar and almost as far as the Wilds. I think that was the inspiration for her fish dish. Tasha knows Tim over at the Equipment Shop needs a break every so often, and what better way to recharge than to get some fishing in? Every Friday, Tim sets sail at the crack of dawn and returns by noon with a barrel full of Ancientscales ready for Tasha to make them into Ancientscale Filets with Tomatillo Crema. So flaky.

As far as the rumors regarding "Buried Pirate Treasure" here at the outpost are concerned, I wouldn't bother. The true treasure to dig up are those beets for the Siren's Gem Salad, both ruby and golden.

THE UNICORN HOUSE ROAST

This roast is a labor of love for Tasha. Once the wild pig is secured from the Merchant Alliance it is carefully transported up the ladders to the tavern. Tasha has dug a pit in the back where she takes great care in roasting this tavern specialty. I personally go to great lengths to get here for Sunday dinner–it's the perfect meal to share with friends accompanied by a very large tankard of grog.

 Easy

 Prep: 10 minutes
Active: 3 hours

 Servings: dependent on size of roast

INGREDIENTS

- 1 x 6–8 lbs bone-in pre-cooked ham shank

Glaze
- 1 tbsp orange juice
- 2 tbsp pomegranate juice
- ½ cup orange tangerine marmalade
- ½ cup Pineapple Jam (see page 112)
- ¼ cup apple cider vinegar
- 1 tsp vanilla extract
- ¼ cup mustard

1. Preheat oven to 350°F. If the ham is brined, rinse off completely to get rid of salt. Prep the ham by keeping the fat side on top and placing it comfortably in a medium roasting pan. Roast for 90 minutes.

2. In small saucepan over low heat, combine the juices, marmalade, and jam and cook until melted together. Remove from the heat and add the cider vinegar, vanilla, and mustard. Score the top of the ham with a crosshatch pattern and brush with the glaze. Return to the oven and cook for 30 minutes, then brush with glaze. Cook another 20 minutes and then brush with glaze. Return to oven and finish cooking until a thermometer reads 160°F.

3. Remove from the oven and transfer to cutting board, tent with foil and allow to stand for 15 minutes. Place the pan with the juices on the stove (hob) and over a medium heat scrape the bits and cook down to a reduction, then pour into a serving dish and serve with the sliced ham.

ANCIENTSCALE FILLET WITH TOMATILLO CREMA

This dish is both tasty and incredibly satisfying. Tasha adds extra flavor with a tangy tomatillo sauce and serves it with asparagus spears, although she prefers to call them "Cutlass Blades." Our Weaponsmiths haven't forged any spears that we know of just yet.

 Easy   **Prep:** 10 minutes **Inactive:** 30 minutes **Active:** 20 minutes   Serves: 2-4   Pescatarian

1. To make the marinade, blend 1 tbsp oil and the other ingredients together in a food processor, then transfer to a plastic resealable bag or shallow baking dish. Wash and clean the fish fillets and marinate them for a minimum of 30 minutes, but no longer than an hour, flipping them once or twice. Remove the fillets from the marinade.
2. In a cast iron pan, heat 1 tbsp oil and add 2 fillets, cook for 4 minutes on each side. The fish should be flaky with an internal temperature of 140°F. Repeat with remaining fillets. Check for seasoning. Serve with tomatillo crema.

Tomatillo Crema

1. Husk and wash the tomatillos. Using tongs, in a dry skillet, carefully roast the tomatillos and garlic until they have blistered skin. Remove and allow to cool slightly.
2. Add all ingredients to a blender and process till smooth and creamy.

 Easy   **Prep:** 5 minutes **Active:** 20 minutes   Servings: varies   Vegetarian

CUTLASS BLADES

 Moderate   **Prep:** 5 minutes **Active:** 10 minutes   Serves 2-4   Vegan

1. Clean the asparagus and trim off the bottom third. In a large bowl, add water and ice cubes to make an ice bath. Set aside.
2. Add 6 cups water, the lemon juice, and salt to a medium to large pot. Bring to boil and add the asparagus. Cook for 2–3 minutes. Remove quickly and add to the ice bath to shock the asparagus. Serve with melted butter.

FILLET INGREDIENTS

- 2 tbsp coconut oil
- 1 tbsp agave syrup
- ¼ cup lime juice
- ¼ cup orange juice
- ¼ cup olive oil
- 1 chipotle pepper
- ¼ tsp salt
- 4 mahi mahi fillets

CREMA INGREDIENTS

- 6 tomatillos
- 2 garlic cloves
- 1 bunch or 1 cup of cilantro (coriander)
- 1 tbsp lime juice
- ¼ cup Mexican crema
- ¼ cup mayo
- 1 tsp salt

CUTLASS INGREDIENTS

- 1 bunch asparagus
- Juice from 1 lemon
- 1 tsp salt
- Melted butter

THE SIREN'S GEMS SALAD

The Siren's Gems are a thing of beauty as much as they are valuable. This roasted beet salad seeks to answer the riddle: if Siren's Gems were found in the ground like hidden treasure, what would they be? Yar, glorious, shimmering beets they be!

 Easy

 Prep: 3 hours
Active: 15 minutes

 Serves 2

 Vegetarian

1. Preheat the oven to 450°F. Make sure the beets are the same size. Using rubber or plastic gloves wash, clean, and cut off each end of the beets. Using a small knife, pierce the beets multiple times to let the steam out and place them in a medium roasting dish. Add ½ inch of water to the bottom of the dish. Drizzle 2 tbsp oil and 1 tsp salt on the beets. Cover the dish with foil and roast for 50–55 minutes or until the beets are tender.

2. Carefully remove the dish from the oven, allow to cool for 2 hours then, using gloves, remove the skins. Cut the beets into small pieces and set aside. In a large salad bowl, add the arugula, pistachios, 2 tbsp orange oil, and the vinegar, along with a dash of salt and pepper. Toss to coat. Arrange beets on the bed of arugula. Add the goat's cheese and finish with a drizzle of orange oil, balsamic, and finishing salt and pepper.

INGREDIENTS

- 2 medium red beets
- 2 medium yellow beets
- Kosher salt (flaky sea salt)
- Handful arugula (rocket)
- 2 oz chopped pistachio nuts
- 4 tbsp Orange-Infused Olive Oil (see page 12)
- 4 tbsp coconut balsamic vinegar
- 1 tsp salt and fresh cracked pepper
- 2 oz goat's cheese
- Finishing salt

CAPTAIN BRIGGSY'S BLACK BEANS AND PLANTAINS

Always longing to go on great adventures like her hero Captain Briggsy, Tasha created these with that same spirit, an adventurous dish that can sneak up on you as it has both a sweet and spicy side.

 Easy

 Prep: 10 minutes
Inactive: 1 hour
Active: 40 minutes

 Serves 4

 Vegan

For the Beans

1. In a dry skillet over low to medium heat, toast the garlic cloves until blistered. Set aside, cool, peel, and slice in half. Turn heat down to low and toss in ground cumin, coriander and chipotle powder and toast till fragrant, about 30 seconds. Remove the pan from heat and transfer the spices to bowl and cool.

2. Drain and rinse the black beans. In a small Dutch oven, over medium heat, add the coconut oil and heat till melted. Add onion, cook until translucent. Add the beans, mix with the onion, and cook for 2 minutes. Add the spices and garlic, mix, and cook for another 2 minutes. Add coconut water and water and bring to a boil, reduce heat and simmer uncovered for 20 minutes or until half the liquid has evaporated.

3. Remove from the heat, add half the contents, the garlic pieces and lime juice to a blender, carefully process until smooth and then return to pot. Add salt and cilantro, mix, cover and allow to stand for 1 hour. To serve, reheat and plate with plantains.

For the Plantains

1. Remove the plantain skins. Cut the ripe plantains in diagonal slices. Heat the oil in cast iron skillet. When hot, add the plantain slices and fry each side until caramelized, roughly 2 minutes each side.

2. Remove and drain on paper towels, set aside. When ready to serve, sprinkle with finishing salt.

INGREDIENTS

- 4 roasted garlic cloves
- 1 tsp ground cumin
- 1 tsp ground coriander
- ½ tsp chipotle powder
- 2 x 16-oz cans black beans
- ½ medium white onion, chopped
- 2 tbsp lime juice
- 2 tbsp chopped cilantro (coriander)

- 2 cups coconut water
- 1 cup water
- 1 tbsp coconut oil
- 1 tsp salt

For the Plantains
- 2 very ripe, blackened plantains
- ¼ cup canola (rapeseed) oil
- Finishing salt

MANGO MOUSSE

This is where I truly shine in my contributions to Sea of Thieves fine cuisine. Tasha needed mangoes cut and I contributed my expertise to the two desserts on The Unicorn's menu. Doing my part, one mango at a time.

 Easy   **Prep:** 10 minutes **Inactive:** 4 hours **Active:** 10 minutes   Serves 4   Vegetarian

INGREDIENTS

- ¼ cup cream of coconut
- 1 cup heavy (double) cream (very cold)
- ½ tsp coconut extract
- 1 cup chopped mango (fresh or frozen and defrosted is fine)
- 1 tbsp lime juice
- Extra chopped mango for topping
- 1 tsp lime juice
- Zest of 1 lime
- 1 tbsp coconut palm sugar

1. In a blender, add the cream of coconut from the can and blend till smooth. Set aside. In a large bowl, using an electric mixer, whip the heavy cream and coconut extract until stiff peaks form. Set aside. Combine the mango with lime juice and ¼ cup of the cream of coconut in the blender and process on high for 1–2 minutes until it is a smooth puree.

2. Pour half of the mango puree mixture into the whipped cream and, using a spatula, fold in very gently, making sure to scrape the sides and slowly incorporate the mixtures. Repeat with the remaining mango puree until everything is incorporated.

3. Divide the mixture between 4 small glasses, then refrigerate at least 4 hours before serving. Add the chopped mango and 1 tsp lime juice to a small bowl and mix. Top the mousse with the mango and lime zest, and sprinkle with coconut palm sugar.

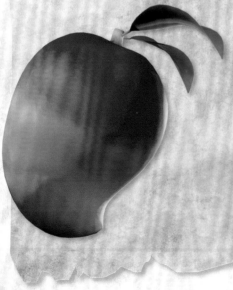

LARINNA'S GRILLED MANGO

As I look out over the sea from atop Ancient Spire, I'm reminded of the abundance of mango and coconut trees these Ancient Isles have to offer. What better way to watch the hot sun dip into the cool ocean than to bring hot and cold into balance with my signature dessert.

 Easy

 Prep: 15 minutes
Active: 10 minutes

 Serves 2

 Vegan

1. Skin the mangoes, being extra careful as they are slippery. Slice the mangoes down the middle around the large pit so that you end up with two large halves. You can also use a mango slicer for this step. Brush one side of the mangoes lightly with agave syrup and set aside.

2. Oil grill grates and, over indirect heat, grill the side with no agave first for about 2 minutes, then flip and grill until there are grill marks, about 2 more minutes. Remove and add to a plate. Sprinkle the mangoes with lime juice, salt, and chili powder if desired. Serve warm with Coconut Ice Cream (see below).

INGREDIENTS

- 2 very ripe mangoes
- 1 tbsp agave syrup
- Vegetable oil
- 2 lime wedges
- Finishing salt
- Chipotle chili powder (optional)

COCONUT ICE CREAM

 Moderate

 Prep: 10 minutes
Inactive: 3 hours
Active: 1 hour

 2 Quarts

 Vegetarian

1. Whisk the egg yolks and sugar together until light and fluffy, and set aside. Toast the coconut in a pan to caramelize lightly. Do not over-toast. Set aside to cool. Combine all the liquid ingredients and vanilla in a medium saucepan and, over medium heat, cook but do not boil, constantly stirring, about 5–7 minutes. Remove from heat.

2. Using a ladle, slowly pour into the egg mixture while whisking, to temper the egg mixture. Once the mixture is warm, pour back into medium saucepan and mix. Over medium heat and stirring constantly, cook for 5 minutes or until back of spatula can be coated. Remove from heat and pour through fine mesh strainer into large bowl. Add ¾ cup toasted coconut to the hot mixture and mix. Set aside to cool for 15 minutes. Cover the custard surface with plastic wrap and refrigerate for 3 or more hours.

3. Pour into ice cream machine, add remaining coconut and churn for 25 minutes. Place in container and freeze.

ICE CREAM INGREDIENTS

- 6 large egg yolks
- ½ cup sugar
- 1 cup sweetened
  coconut flakes
- 1 cup whole milk

- 1 cup coconut milk
- 1 cup cream of coconut
- 2 cups heavy
  (double) cream
- ½ tsp vanilla extract

Special equipment: Ice cream maker

THE GOLD HOARDER

Gold. Gold. Gold. And more gold.

1. In a drink shaker, add the golden rum, lime juice, mango juice, orgeat syrup, and blood orange liqueur. Stir.

2. Pour over large ice cube in an 8-oz glass, top off with dark rum, and garnish with what Gold Hoarders love best–gold!

INGREDIENTS

- 1 oz golden rum
- ½ oz lime juice
- 1 oz mango juice
- ½ oz orgeat syrup
- ½ oz blood orange liqueur
- 1 oz dark rum
- Gold leaf

MANGO TANGO

Selling Chests of Legends at Ancient Spire is a swabbie's task indeed. If you choose not to sell to the Sovereigns then this drink is essential as it will give you the energy and will to live after your fourth, fifth, sixth trip up that ladder.

1. Add all the ingredients except the coconut pulp to a blender and process on high for 1 minute.
2. Add the pulp to the bottom of two goblets and pour mango blend over pulp. Serve with a drink spoon.

INGREDIENTS

- 6 oz mango juice
- 6 oz coconut milk
- 4 oz coconut water
- 1 tsp coconut palm sugar
- 2 oz lime juice
- 1 tbsp coconut pulp

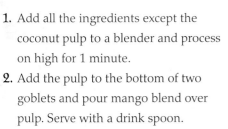

THE WILDS

Adventure awaits a courageous pirate here in the Wilds!

With its overcast skies, greenish-yellow seas, misty atmosphere, and rocky and desolate landscape, it's easy to see why the Order of Souls has an affinity for this region. The islands are wrought with skeletons of deceased pirates, ocean creatures, and shipwrecked vessels. While the flora is scorched and wilted, and fresh resources are scarce, taverns in the Wilds take advantage of indigenous Wildsplashes, wild pigs, snakes, pineapples, and the occasional Kraken.

Teri is the tavern-keeper at **The Snake Pit** over at Dagger Tooth Outpost, one of two taverns in the Wilds. Teri is quite the drinker; she's keen on trying every grog that gets delivered and every grog she serves. She's made certain the Pit has some great dishes, though—the Snake Special I hear is ssssucculent. The second tavern in the region is the **Broken Tusk** over at Galleon's Grave, and it's run by Tess—she's a grog expert and a true culinary explorer. If your voyages are taking you into the Devil's Roar or to the Shores of Gold, stop in and try her Ocean Crawlers in the Sand or the delicious Broken Tusk Tavern Sandwich. Pirates have killed and plundered for less.

THE SNAKE PIT

Dagger Tooth Outpost has large, imposing rock formations that tower over everything, including the Snake Pit tavern, which is prominently positioned at the center of the island, nestled in the large jagged rock. The tavern-keeper here is named Teri and she is quite the pirate. If rumors are to be believed she may have had a liaison with Merrick at some point, but for the most part she passes the time drinking her own grog to try to make the Wilds a little less depressing, I gather. It's true, Chef Hendrick's training sessions with Teri took a bit longer than expected; there was, after all, a lot of slurring. Eventually she was able to craft a menu with some help from Winnie, Sandra, and the Mysterious Stranger.

Winnie over at the Weaponsmith shop, being best pirate friends with Whitney over at Plunder, heard about the tantalizing dishes they had devised with Chef Hendrick's help, and so she wanted the Snake Pit to have the same. Winnie helped Teri create the Broiled Wildsplash served with Order of Souls Potatoes, which came out divine. Sandra, well, that is a tale, a Kraken-killing tale. She thought, what better dish to have on the menu than fried Kraken Rings. And while all these were indeed delicious, the masterpiece came from the Mysterious Stranger himself, creating a meat pie that would warm any pirate's soul as they prepared to take on one of his voyages, for his quests are designed for pirates with a full belly and who are not faint of heart.

MYSTERIOUS STRANGER TAVERN PIE

Waking up in a tavern and looking around, it's most likely the Mysterious Stranger you see first. The dark, quiet type, in the back, very mysterious. He doesn't exactly radiate warmth. But when Teri needed help crafting a meal fit for future pirate legends, well he stepped out of the shadows to create a meat pie that has warmth and character, with the most delicate and flaky of crusts and the most savory of fillings. Slated to become legendary.

 Easy

 Prep: 10 minutes
Inactive: 1–24 hours
Active: 30–40 minutes

 Serve 4

Pie Crust

1. In a large bowl, combine 2 cups flour and the salt. Mix in the butter and lard with a fork or your hands until it feels like sand. In a small bowl, beat the egg yolk with a whisk and add to the flour mix. Add the seltzer water 1 tbsp at a time and mix until dough comes together into a ball.

2. Split into four equal pieces. Flatten each out into a disk and wrap in plastic wrap. Refrigerate for 24 hours. When ready to use, dust flour on a work surface and roll out each disk to fit in 6 ½-inch pie dishes.

(continued on next page)

INGREDIENTS

Pie Crust
- 2 ½ cups all-purpose (plain) flour
- ½ tsp sea salt
- ½ cup cold butter, cut into small pieces
- ½ cup cold lard, cut into small pieces
- 1 large egg yolk
- 3 tbsp cold seltzer (sparkling) water

Filling
- 4 tbsp butter
- 2 tbsp coconut oil
- 1 lb ground pork
- 1 lb ground veal
- ½ cup leek, finely sliced
- ½ cup celery, finely chopped
- 2 tbsp tomato paste
- 1 ½ cups beef stock
- 1 tsp salt
- 1 tsp ground pepper
- Marauder's Mash (see page 24)

Filling

1. Preheat the oven to 350°F. Place 4 pie dishes on parchment paper-covered cookie sheet and set aside. Combine 1 tbsp butter and 1 tbsp coconut oil in large skillet on high heat. Brown the meat in batches so it doesn't get too watery, then set aside in a bowl. Reduce heat to medium and add 1 tbsp butter and 1 tbsp coconut oil to the pan and cook the leek and celery until soft, about 5 minutes.

2. Add the cooked meat, the tomato paste, and stock, stir well, and bring to a boil, then reduce to low and simmer for 15 minutes. Test for seasoning, add salt and pepper to taste, then continue cooking for another 5 minutes until most of the liquid is absorbed.

3. Add the filling to the pie shells, cover with mashed potatoes and hash with a fork. Melt 2 tbsp butter and brush on top of the potatoes. Place the cookie sheet with pies in the oven and bake for 45–50 minutes until the top is golden brown. Serve hot with a sauce of your choice.

SNAKE SPECIAL

It's not tough getting snake meat in the Wilds, they tend to pop up all over these rocky shores. But cooking them can be challenging. They need plenty of time to braise and turn fork tender. This recipe does take extra time, but it's well worth it. When done the meat practically slithers off the bone.

 Easy

 Prep: 5 minutes
Inactive: 4 hours
Active: 20 minutes

 Serves 4

1. Add the onion and ginger to a cookie sheet and char in the oven under the broiler (grill). Remove and set aside. Add the coconut oil to large Dutch oven and on medium heat, brown the tails in batches on all sides. Remove and set aside.

2. Add the spices and garlic to the pan and cook for 2 minutes until fragrant. Add the tails, onion, and ginger to the pot, arrange and then add all liquids and the sugar to the pot. Bring to boil, reduce heat to a simmer, and cover to cook on low for 4 hours until tender and falling off the bone. Remove lid and cook for another 20 minutes or until liquid is reduced and meat is glazed. Serve with Coconut Rice (see page 24).

INGREDIENTS

- 1 small yellow onion, quartered
- 1 x 3-inch-thick slice of fresh ginger, split in half
- 1 tbsp coconut oil
- 3 lbs oxtails, with lots of meat on them
- 4 pieces star anise
- 3 black cardamon pods
- 3 cloves
- 2 bay leaves
- 6 cloves garlic, peeled and smashed
- 12 oz Jamaican ginger beer
- 5 tbsp soy sauce
- Water to cover, 8 cups
- 1 tbsp coconut palm sugar
- Salt (to taste)

BROILED WILDSPLASH

Firm and flaky, with a crispy skin, simply a delicious preparation of the regional Wildsplash. It seems Winnie took inspiration for this meal from both the sea and the Order of Souls, explaining the very purple hue these potatoes have.

 Easy   **Prep:** 10 minutes **Active:** 15 minutes   Serves 4   Pescatarian

1. Set an oven rack on the center rung. Preheat the broiler (grill). In a small bowl, whisk together the preserves, vinegar, parsley, red pepper, garlic, and salt, then set aside.

2. Lightly sprinkle the fillets with salt. Heat the oil in cast iron pan over medium heat. Once hot, place the fillets in pan, skin side down. They will shrink. Cook for 4 minutes. Add 1 tsp sauce over the fleshy part of fish and place the pan in the oven under the broiler. Cook for 5 minutes. Carefully remove, place on Order of Souls Potatoes and finish with lemon zest and flaky salt.

ORDER OF SOULS POTATOES

 Easy   **Prep:** 10 minutes **Active:** 1 hour   Servings: varies   Vegan

1. Preheat oven to 400°F. In a large pot, add 3 quarts of water and 1 tbsp of kosher salt. Wash, peel, and cut the potatoes and add them to pot. Bring to a boil, then parboil for 5 minutes. Drain the potatoes, transfer them to a large bowl, and toss with oil.

2. Lay the potatoes on a cookie sheet. Using the back of a large spoon, press down on each potato, smashing them. Season with zest, onion, parsley, and chili powder. Transfer to the oven and roast for about 20 minutes until crispy. Remove from oven, transfer to a medium bowl and, using a fork, mash potatoes completely. Add the coconut cream and butter and continue blending till smooth. Finish with flaky salt.

WILDSPLASH INGREDIENTS

- 3 tbsp pineapple preserves
- 2 tbsp rice vinegar
- 1 tsp chopped fresh parsley
- ⅛ tsp crushed red pepper
- 1 garlic clove, minced
- 4 x 6-oz striped sea
  bass fillets or other
  white flaky fish
- ¼ tsp salt
- 1 tbsp coconut oil
- Zest of 1 lemon
- Finishing salt

POTATOES INGREDIENTS

- 3 lbs purple sweet potatoes
- 1 tbsp kosher salt (flaky sea salt)
- 2 tbsp olive oil
- 1 tsp lemon zest
- 1 tsp granulated onion
- 1 tsp dried parsley
- ¼ tsp chipotle or guajillo chili powder
- 2 tbsp coconut cream
- 3 tbsp plant butter
- Flaky finishing salt

KRAKEN RINGS WITH AIOLI

Sandra the shipwright encountered a Kraken and lived to tell the tale, and she is now set on revenge preparing a worthy vessel to hunt it down. The Snake Pit serves pirates from time to time who've vanquished a few Krakens and have meat to sell. Sandra figured this dish would keep her energized and focused on her goal. True, but it's also delicious.

 Easy

 Prep: 30 minutes
Inactive: 1 hour
Active: 1 hour

 Serves 2

 Pescatarian

1. In a medium bowl, mix together the buttermilk and coconut milk and add the Kraken pieces, making sure to coat the Kraken completely. Refrigerate for 1 hour. In a large bowl, combine the dry ingredients.
2. Heat the oil in a Dutch oven or heavy pot to 375°F. Drain the Kraken pieces from the milk and add them to the flour blend in batches. Toss and coat them. Add the Kraken to the oil and fry until golden brown, roughly 3–4 minutes. Remove with strainer and transfer to a paper towel-lined tray to drain. Season with salt. Serve immediately with chopped parsley, limes, and aioli.

Aioli

1. In a small fry pan over low-medium heat, roast the garlic cloves with skins on until soft, about 10 minutes. Keep a close eye on them and do not allow them to burn. Remove from heat and allow to cool, then remove the skins.
2. Smash the garlic in a small bowl, making sure no whole pieces are left. Add lime juice and salt, mix. Add the remaining ingredients and mix well. Season to taste.

INGREDIENTS

- 1 lb Kraken (or squid, cleaned, rinsed, and cut into rings, including tentacles)
- ½ cup buttermilk
- ½ cup coconut milk
- 1 ½ cups flour
- 2 tsp cornstarch (cornflour)
- 1 tsp garlic powder
- 1 tsp chipotle powder
- 1 tsp salt
- ½ tsp black pepper
- 2 ½ cups canola oil
- Fresh parsley
- Limes

Aioli
- 4 large garlic cloves
- 1 tbsp lime juice
- 1 cup Homemade Mayo (see page 11)
- 1 tsp agave syrup
- 1 tsp coconut aminos
- Salt and pepper

SEARED OCEAN CRAWLERS IN THE SAND

 Easy **Prep:** 10 minutes **Active:** 20 minutes Serves 4 Shellfish

1. In a small saucepan, whisk together the syrup, sake, mirin, soy sauce, lime juice, and pineapple jam. Heat up and add 2 tbsp of the butter. Simmer and continue to cook until reduced and thick.

2. Lightly salt the scallops on both sides. In a large fry pan, heat the oil and 4 tbsp butter. Sear half the scallops on 1 side for 3–4 minutes, basting them with the melted butter in the pan. Flip the scallops and sear for another 4 minutes while basting. Serve with a drizzle of pineapple sauce reduction over Teri's Pearls Couscous.

INGREDIENTS

- 2 tsp agave syrup
- 1 tbsp sake
- 1 tbsp mirin
- 2 tsp soy sauce
- 1 tbsp lime juice
- 1 tbsp pineapple jam
- 6 tbsp butter
- 1 lb large scallops
- ½ tsp salt
- 1 tbsp coconut oil

TERI'S PEARLS COUSCOUS

 Easy **Prep:** 10 minutes **Inactive:** 5 minutes **Active:** 15 minutes Serves 4 Vegan

1. Toast the pistachios in a dry pan till fragrant and set aside. In a medium saucepan, fry the couscous in the oil and butter until nutty brown, about 1 minute. Add 1 ½ cups water and salt to the couscous and bring to a boil, then reduce to simmer and cover for 15–20 minutes. Remove from heat and allow to stand for 5 minutes.

2. Add the pistachios and lemon juice, fluff and serve with chopped mint.

INGREDIENTS

- ¼ cup roasted pistachios, chopped
- 1 cup pearl couscous
- ½ tbsp plant butter
- ½ tbsp canola (rapeseed) oil
- Salt
- 1 tsp lemon juice
- 1 tsp chopped mint

PINEAPPLE UPSIDE DOWN CAKE

Using only your trusty cast iron pan, this treat can be made even in your ship's galley. You just need those pineapples and pomegranates to get you started, and maybe some strong grog to flip it.

 Easy

 Prep: 15 minutes
Active: 1 hour

 Serves 6–8

 Dairy free

1. Preheat the oven to 350°F. Lightly butter a #8 (9-inch) cast iron pan. Add the brown sugar to the bottom of the pan. Melt the butter and pour over the top of the brown sugar, blend and spread over the entire pan. Place the pineapple rings on top and add the pomegranate seeds to the center of the rings.

2. In a large bowl, whisk the flour, baking soda, powder, and salt together and set aside. In another large bowl, cream the coconut oil, butter, and palm sugar together for about 2 minutes. Add the eggs one at a time and continue to cream the mixture. Add the extracts and pineapple juice. Whisk this mixture into the flour. Whisk in the coconut milk until everything is blended and smooth.

3. Pour the batter over the pineapple slices and bake for 30–40 minutes until a cake tester comes out clean. Let it cool. Place a cake plate on top of cake and then flip carefully and remove pan.

INGREDIENTS

The topping
- ½ cup packed dark brown sugar
- ¼ cup plant butter
- 4 cored pineapple slices
- Pomegranate seeds

The cake
- 1 ½ cups cake flour
- 1 tsp baking powder
- ¼ tsp baking (bicarbonate) soda
- ½ tsp salt
- 3 tbsp vegetable butter
- 3 tbsp solidified coconut oil
- ¾ cup coconut palm sugar
- 2 large eggs
- ½ tsp vanilla extract
- ½ tsp coconut extract
- 2 tbsp pineapple juice
- ½ cup coconut milk

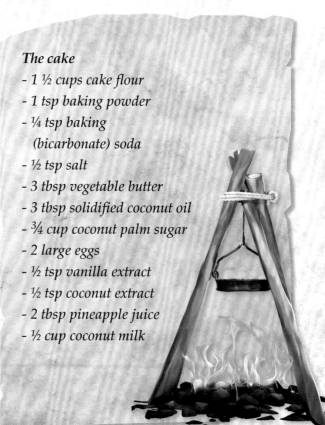

THE REAPER

Dark, fiery, and sneaky. Just like a Reaper. This chocolatey, spicy, coffee beverage can have the heat sneak up on you if you are not prepared. Keep the spyglass handy. If you see yourself as a level five Reaper, add more chilis.

1. Add 6 cups water, ¼ cup sugar, cinnamon, and anise pods to a saucepan and bring to a boil. Stir to make sure the sugar has melted completely. Remove from the heat. Add the coffee, stir, cover, and let steep for 8 minutes.

2. Meanwhile, in a small saucepan over low heat, bring the chocolate, 1 tbsp sugar, milk, cream, Thai chilis, and dash of salt to a light simmer, making sure all the chocolate is incorporated into the milk. Remove from heat. Let steep for 1 minute or more. Remove the chilis and pour chocolate into a carafe or coffee pot. Pour the coffee through a strainer over the chocolate, mix and serve.

INGREDIENTS

- 8 tbsp ground dark roast Jamaican coffee
- ¼ cup plus 1 tbsp coconut palm sugar
- 4 cinnamon sticks
- 2 star anise pods
- 2 tbsp double Dutch dark chocolate powder (cocoa powder)
- 2 Thai chilis
- ½ cup coconut milk
- ½ cup cream
- Dash of salt

SNAKE VENOM

This drink may or may not make you see purple–just depends how much you drink.

1. Place salt on a flat plate and, using a lime, moisten the rim of glass. Dip the glass into the salt either halfway or all round, depending on taste. Add one very large or a few smaller ice cubes to the glass. Add ice to a mixer, along with the tequila, lime juice, and blue curacao. Shake well and pour into glass.

2. Using a shot glass with the grenadine, slowly add to the top of the drink and watch as the purple snake venom seeps into your glass.

INGREDIENTS

- 1 tbsp black salt
- 2 oz tequila blanco
- 2 oz lime juice
- 1 oz blue curacao
- ½ oz grenadine
- 1 lime slice

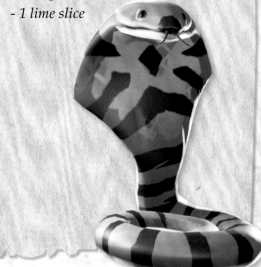

THE BROKEN TUSK

The Broken Tusk tavern can be found at Galleon's Grave Outpost at the end of the main dock, framed by two large rock formations cradling the remains of a galleon ship high above the ground. The island is truly a grave of broken ships and creatures' bones. The tavern-keeper at the Broken Tusk is Tess, and she's an expert in all things grog, from a variety of specialty brews to making her own, such as Tess's Dawn Amber, which happens to be one of her favorite banana-based grog recipes. When Chef Hendrick arrived, Tess was ready. She started to imagine all the grog and food pairings that could be created. Some of the residents here, like Trevor from the equipment shop and Henry the Hoarder, swear by Tess's true masterpiece, which oddly enough is not her grog but the Broken Tusk Tavern Sandwich. It's simply perfect if you ask them, and I tend to agree.

Of course, with pineapple as the main influence in this region, Tess put together a menu that brings the fruit to life. From Pork and Pineapple Tacos to Pineapple Beignets, pirates shouldn't consider leaving until they've tried everything on the menu, paired with a variety of grogs of course.

THE BROKEN TUSK TAVERN SANDWICH

When you wake up at Galleon's Grave, before you run out and loot every barrel at the outpost, make sure you get your order in for one of the best sandwiches a pirate has ever tasted. Sure, it takes Tess the whole day to make, but it's worth more than that logbook glinting at you just over the dock. Remember, there are barrels at the very top here, so fuel up!

 Easy

 Prep: 10 minutes
Inactive: 8 hours
Active: 15 minutes

 Servings: varies

1. Salt the short ribs with the kosher salt. Heat the coconut oil in pan or in bottom of slow cooker, insert (if your slow cooker model allows) and brown each side of the ribs in batches and set aside. Slice the onion and add slices to the bottom of the slow cooker. Add the sugar, thyme, and pomegranate syrup to the top of the onions. Place the ribs on top of the onions, then add the cider and beef stock.

2. Cover and cook on low for 8 hours, checking every 2 hours and turning the ribs and mixing the braising liquid. After 8 hours, remove the ribs and allow to cool. Wrap the ribs and store in the fridge. Strain 1 cup braising liquid into a glass mason jar for reheating, seal, and store in the fridge.

Sandwich Construction

1. Using one rib per sandwich, shred the meat into large chunks. Remove solidified fat from top of braising liquid in the jar and discard. Add 2 tbsp braising liquid to a small frying pan over medium heat. Add the short rib chunks and heat through, about 1–3 minutes.

2. In the meantime, prepare two slices of white country bread with mayonnaise and lettuce. Place the warm rib meat on the lettuce, season with salt and pepper to taste, top with a second piece of bread, cut, and serve.

INGREDIENTS

- 4–4 ½ lbs boneless beef short ribs
- 1 tbsp kosher salt (flaky sea salt)
- 2 tbsp coconut oil
- 1 large yellow onion
- 2 tbsp coconut palm sugar
- 2 cups apple cider
- 1 cup beef stock
- 3 tbsp pomegranate syrup
- 1 tsp dried thyme

Special equipment:
Slow cooker

Sandwich
- *White country bread*
- *Lettuce*
- *Homemade Mayo (see page 11)*
- *Salt and pepper*

PENDRAGON'S BBQ CHICKEN PIZZA

Sir Arthur Pendragon, captain of the shipwrecked Blackwyche, champion of the Order of Souls, and a pirate with really bad luck. As with most of his quests, this pizza has multiple steps, takes some time, but ultimately delivers pure satisfaction.

 Complex

 Prep: 1 hour
Inactive: 24 hours +1 hour
Active: 40 minutes

 Serves 6

 Omit chicken for a vegetarian pizza

Dough

1. In a large bowl, whisk together the dry ingredients. Add warm water and mix together with your hands or a spatula until all ingredients are combined. Cover the bowl with plastic wrap and set in a warm place to rise for 24 hours. If it's too cold where you are, place the bowl in an unheated oven to rise.
2. When ready to make pie, transfer the dough to a floured surface and knead into a large smooth dough ball. Using olive oil, grease a smaller bowl and add the dough. Cover with plastic and allow to sit and rise for another hour at room temperature.

Tandoori Chicken Thighs

1. Mix all the spices to make the tandoori spice mix. In a medium bowl, mix the yogurt and spice mix together. In a shallow baking dish or large resealable bag, combine the chicken thighs and yogurt mixture. Marinate in a refrigerator for at least 2 hours.
2. Preheat the oven to 400°F. Remove the chicken from the marinade, wipe off excess yogurt, and place in a shallow baking dish, keeping the pieces as separated as possible. Bake for 30 minutes or until internal temperature reaches 170°F. Transfer to a plate and allow to cool completely, then refrigerate for use on pizza later. Use any remaining chicken in sandwiches or salads.

Pizza

1. Set the oven rack to the bottom of the oven. Preheat oven to 500–550°F. This should take about 30 minutes. Transfer the dough ball to a lightly floured surface and roll out just enough to get a round disk. Lightly oil the bottom of a pizza pan. Transfer the dough disk to the pan and stretch it out to the edges. Pierce with a fork and transfer to oven for 5 minutes.
2. Remove from the oven. Layer BBQ sauce, onion, cheeses, chicken, pineapple, and cilantro and return to the oven and cook for 7–11 minutes until the crust is crispy. Remove from oven, let cool for 3 minutes, slice, and enjoy.

INGREDIENTS

Dough
- 2 cups all-purpose (plain) flour
- ½ tsp instant yeast
- 2 tsp salt
- ¾ cup warm water
- 1 tsp olive oil

Tandoori Chicken Thighs
- 1 tsp each: paprika, ground ginger, coriander, ground cumin, ground cardamon, garlic powder
- ½ tsp turmeric
- ½ tsp salt
- ¼ tsp chipotle chili powder
- 1 cup plain coconut yogurt
- 8 boneless, skinless chicken thighs

Pizza
- ¾ cup Pendragon's BBQ sauce (see page 12)
- ¼ cup red onion sliced
- 1 cup shredded mozzarella cheese
- ¾ cup shredded smoked gouda
- 1 cup cooked tandoori chicken, shredded
- ½ cup pineapple chunks
- 1 tbsp chopped cilantro (coriander)

PORK AND PINEAPPLE TACOS

While testing Aged Grog pairings, Tess found that wild pigs and pineapples have a perfect flavor profile when cooked together. Thankfully, she didn't decide to make it into another one of her self-brew grog recipes–we all think that the two taste much better together in tacos.

 Easy

 Prep: 10 minutes
Inactive: 24 hours
Active: 2.5 hours

 Serves 12

 Gluten free

1. Combine all ingredients except the pineapple, cilantro, onions and limes. Marinate the pork for at least 2 hours, preferably overnight.
2. Preheat the oven to 300°F and place an oven rack on a low setting, making sure to provide enough height for the baking sheet and skewer. Wrap the baking sheet in foil and place a skewer stand on top. Build the stack on the skewer, starting with two pineapple slices followed by all the pork slices, finish with two or more pineapple slices.
3. Bake for 2–2-½ hours or until the internal temperature of the pork is 150–160°F. Remove and let sit for 10 minutes, then proceed to carve off pieces. Serve with tortillas and top with cilantro, pickled onions, and lime.

INGREDIENTS

- 5 lbs boneless pork shoulder, sliced into steak-sized pieces
- 3 tbsp achiote paste
- 2 tbsp guajillo chili powder
- 1 tbsp garlic powder
- 1 tbsp oregano
- 1 tbsp cumin
- 1 tsp coriander powder
- 1 tbsp salt
- 1 tsp pepper
- 1 tsp chipotle powder
- ¾ cup apple cider vinegar
- 1 cup pineapple juice
- 1 pineapple, sliced
- Corn tortillas
- Cilantro (coriander)
- Pickled Onions (see page 10)
- Lime wedges

Special equipment:
Meat skewer

PINEAPPLE RICE

Every so often the Merchant Alliance gets wind of a ship that has specialty cargo in the area, which doesn't happen too often. When Tess hears of the possibility of rice being aboard, she enlists some able-bodied pirates to "influence" the course of that ship. As a Bilge Rat myself, working the black market, I can say I have no knowledge of such things.

 Easy
 Prep: 10 minutes
Inactive: 25 minutes
Active: 30 minutes
 Serves 4
 Vegan

1. Add the rice to a heatproof bowl and cover with boiling water. Let stand for 15 minutes. Drain through a mesh sieve and allow to stand while heating the oil in medium saucepan over medium heat. Transfer rice to pan and fry the rice until nutty and all oil is absorbed. Add the salt and pineapple and continue stirring a minute longer, combining ingredients.

2. Make sure the stock and pineapple juice add up to two cups, then add both along with butter, lime juice, and agave syrup to the pot. Stir and bring to a boil, reduce to a simmer, cover, and let cook for 15 minutes undisturbed. Take off stove and let stand for 10 minutes. Uncover, fluff, and mix in chopped cilantro and green onions.

BROKEN TUSK CURRY

Sometimes you just want a meal that satisfies a hearty pirate appetite. One that is warm and balanced and can help you take on some rocky shores. This curry is sure to satisfy even the saltiest of pirates.

 Easy
 Prep: 30 minutes
Active: 35 minutes
 Serves 4
 Vegan
Diary free

1. In a Dutch oven over medium heat, add the coconut oil. Cook the onion for 3 minutes and add in the minced garlic. Cook for 1 more minute. Add in the sweet potato and parsnips and ½ tsp of salt. Cook for 2 minutes, then add the curry powder, Thai chili, ½ tsp salt, and turmeric and cook for another 3 minutes.

2. Add the coconut milk, soy sauce, and aminos and cook for another three minutes. Add the bell pepper, coconut water, and vegetable stock, bring to a boil, cover, and simmer for 15 minutes, covered.

3. Check the vegetables are cooked. Add black-eyed peas and peas, mix, and cook for five minutes. Serve with rice and top with plain coconut yogurt and pomegranate seeds.

RICE INGREDIENTS

- 1 cup long grain rice
- 1 tbsp coconut oil
- 1 tsp sea salt
- 1 cup crushed pineapple, drained
- 1 cup pineapple juice
- 1 cup vegetable stock
- 2 tbsp vegan butter
- Juice of ½ lime
- 2 tsp agave syrup
- Cilantro (coriander), chopped
- 1 green (spring) onion, chopped

CURRY INGREDIENTS

- 2 tbsp coconut oil
- 1 small yellow onion
- 3 cloves garlic, minced
- 1 Japanese sweet
  potato, cubed
- 2 large parsnips, sliced
- 1 tsp salt
- 2 tsp curry powder
- 1 tsp Thai chilis, chopped
- ½ tsp ground turmeric
- 2 cups coconut milk
- 1 tsp soy sauce
- 1 tsp coconut aminos
- ½ cup chopped green
  bell pepper
- 1 cup coconut water
- 1 cup vegetable stock
- 1 x 15-oz can of
  black-eyed peas (beans),
  rinsed and drained
- 1 cup frozen peas
- Plain coconut yogurt
- Pomegranate seeds

ROOTS OF THE ANCIENTS

The Ancients have extensive history and lore in the Sea of Thieves, above and below the sea. From the Veil of the Ancients to the Shroudbreaker and the Merfolk alliance, the Ancients have always been and continue to be the roots of this wondrous world.

 Easy

 Prep: 15 minutes
Active: 30 minutes

 Serves 4

 Vegan

1. Peel the vegetables and chop into 1-inch equally sized pieces. In a large sauté pan, add two cups of water and the vegetables. Over medium low heat bring to a simmer.

2. Add agave syrup and butter and cook on a low simmer. Stir occasionally and cook until the vegetables are tender, about 15–20 minutes. Remove the glazed vegetables and finish with salt and chopped sage.

INGREDIENTS

- 3 carrots
- 2 parsnips
- 1 medium golden beet
- 2 tbsp agave syrup
- 2 tbsp plant butter
- 3 large fresh sage leaves
- Salt

PINEAPPLE BEIGNETS

 Easy

 Prep: 5 minutes
Inactive: 10 minutes
Active: 15 minutes

 Serves 8–12

 Vegetarian

INGREDIENTS

- ¾ cup crushed pineapple
- ¾ cup sugar
- 3 large eggs
- 1 tbsp vegetable butter, melted
- ¼ cup milk
- ⅛ tsp allspice
- 2 tsp vanilla extract
- 2 tsp pineapple extract
- 2–3 cups Canola (rapeseed) oil
- 1 ¼ cup all-purpose flour
- 1 tsp baking powder
- ⅛ tsp salt
- Powdered (icing) sugar

1. In a bowl, mix together the pineapple, sugar, eggs, melted butter, milk, allspice, and extracts. In a fryer or deep pan, heat the oil to 375°F. In another large bowl, whisk together the flour, baking powder, and salt. Slowly pour the pineapple mixture into the dry ingredients, then whisk together until well blended. Take care not to overmix.

2. Using a small ice cream scoop, add the batter to the oil. Be mindful of the oil temperature, it will drop or rise, so just make sure the fritters do not burn. The fritters should fluff up as they fry–monitor and flip until golden, about 3–5 minutes. Remove and drain on a paper towel for 1 minute, then serve with powdered sugar and pineapple jam. These fritters will be denser than regular beignets due to the pineapple.

PINEAPPLE JAM

Several crates of fine sugar appeared on the dock recently.
Only one thing to do with that much sugar. Jam.

 Easy

 Prep: 5 minutes
Active: 1 hour
10 minutes

 1 pint

 Vegan

1. Skin, core and chop up the pineapple. Add the pieces to a blender and process for 10 seconds or less–it should be fluid but with chunks in it.

2. Add to a medium saucepan with the coconut water, then simmer on low to medium heat for 30 minutes until the pineapple is soft. Add the sugar and lime juice, mix, and cook on low for 40 minutes or until very thick and bubbly. Transfer to an airtight container and refrigerate.

INGREDIENTS

- 1 pineapple
- 1 cup coconut water
- 2 cups sugar
- 4 tbsp lime juice

SIRENS' TEARS

The Sirens consume our thoughts and actions as we dive into the depths of their shrines in search of gold and adventure...this drink is a sweet homage to the gold we seek, with a touch of the salty sea to remind us of their sorrow.

1. Moisten the rim of a glass with lime juice and add sea salt. In a drink mixer, combine ice cubes and all the ingredients except the blue curacao. Shake well until fully blended.
2. Pour into glass with ice, then finish with blue curacao and optional gold leaf.

INGREDIENTS

- 2 oz good dark rum
- 1 oz fresh lime juice
- 3 oz pineapple juice
- 1 oz coconut water
- 1 oz blue curacao
- Sea salt
- Gold leaf (optional)

GALLEON'S GHOST

With a name like Galleon's Grave, there was bound to be a ghost.

1. In drink shaker, add the mint, ginger slices, sugar, salt, and lime juice. Using a muddler, muddle the ingredients for a minute or so to release the flavor and mix with the lime juice. Add pineapple juice and ice and shake well.

2. Add ice to 2 glasses, and strain half the ingredients into each, including the mint and ginger. Top off with ginger beer and serve with mint leaves.

INGREDIENTS

- *Small bunch fresh mint*
- *2 inches fresh ginger, peeled and sliced*
- *2 tsp brown sugar*
- *¼ tsp sea salt*
- *1 oz fresh lime juice*
- *8 oz pineapple juice*
- *12 oz ginger beer*

THE DEVIL'S ROAR

A pirate never starts out in the Devil's Roar, you must really want to sail here. The journey is wrought with danger and challenges that will give even the most seasoned pirate pause, instinctively causing them to anchor turn right back west. Those pirates that do brave the dark skies, acrid air, molten flying rocks, and fiery embers will be well rewarded, for the quests undertaken here are much more lucrative. This region has one outpost, which has an honorary governess, Grace Morrow, who gives her name to the island Morrow's Peak. She is part of the Forsaken Shores Alliance and has spent most of her time protecting the outpost.

The Charred Parrot is the tavern located at this outpost, and it is run by Tallulah. Pirates come here on their way to the Shores of Gold to take on the grandest of voyages, while dodging active volcanoes along the way. Tallulah likes meeting new pirate explorers as they pass through. She knows they are on a perilous quest and that it's hot out there, so they must load up on refreshing grog before they shove off.

THE CHARRED PARROT

Grace Morrow is the founder and caretaker of Morrow's Peak, which is built around the wreck of her ship, the Shroudbreaker. The island itself is covered in molten rocks, thermal geysers, and a dormant volcano. The Charred Parrot tavern is where you can find a good strong grog poured by its tavern-keeper, Tallulah. It was the last stop on Chef Hendrick's culinary tour, and he made sure to take advantage of what this region is known for, FIRE!

Tallulah gets most of her supplies, especially her grog, from Matilda, the Senior Trader here, who also seems to enjoy the concoctions Tallulah creates, especially the volcano-inspired "Piña Colava." Although upon Chef Hendrick's departure, the Pirate Emporium shopkeeper Elijah was tasked with a scroll of ingredients a cutlass long from Talullah after she heard of Eduardo's ability to find steak for Tanya at The Drowned Rat. With Matilda's help, Tallulah fashioned a grill grate out of iron pieces from the wrecked galleon and began to treat residents and visiting pirates to grilled and charred delicacies from land and sea. The signature house burger is reason alone to traverse the volcano-ridden region and Tallulah hopes you make the trip; she has crates of goodies just waiting to be charred!

TAVERN BURGER WITH PINEAPPLE CHIPOTLE BACON RELISH

Tallulah knows a few adventurous pirates that swear they've seen the Shores of Gold, but more importantly, they are the same pirates that traverse the wider world and source the most delectable ingredients. She has enticed Elijah with several gold pieces to procure the ingredients for the tavern's specialty house burger. Although Tallulah prepares the meat for this dish over a barrel with her cutlass, you might need a grinder.

 Easy

 Prep: 20 minutes
Active: 1 hour

 Serves 6

1. Trim the beef of any silver skin and extra fat or gristle, cut into 1-inch cubes, transfer to a medium bowl and place in the freezer for at least 15 minutes before adding to a meat grinder to produce 2 lbs ground beef blend. Season with cumin and granulated onion, mix together, then form into 6 patties.
2. Making sure patties are at room temperature, season with salt and add to an oiled grill grate. Cook to desired doneness and serve on a bun of choice, top with Pineapple Chipotle Bacon Relish and dress with desired extras.

The Relish

1. In a cast-iron pan, add the oil and heat the bacon until fat is rendered and almost crispy. Add the red onion and cook until it is soft, about 5 minutes. Add pineapple juice and scrape off the bacon bits.
2. Transfer to a small saucepan and add the pineapple, chipotle, vinegar, sugar, and agave syrup and bring to a boil. Reduce heat to a simmer and cook for another 20 minutes until jam like–check for seasoning. Remove from stove and transfer to a bowl to cool.

INGREDIENTS

- ½ lb brisket meat
- 1 lb chuck meat
- ½ lb shortrib meat
- ½ tsp granulated onion
- ½ tsp cumin
- Salt

Special equipment:
Meat grinder

The Relish
- ½ lb bacon, chopped into ½-inch slices
- 1 tbsp coconut oil
- ½ large red onion, sliced
- ½ cup pineapple juice
- 1 cup chopped pineapple
- 1 chipotle pepper, minced
- 1 tbsp brown sugar
- 2 tbsp cider vinegar
- 1 tbsp agave syrup

CHARRED PARROT

With an iron pan over an open flame, the Charred Parrot's namesake meal is easy, quick, and delectable. Best of all, it keeps any feathery pirate friends who drop into the tavern quiet all night.

 Easy

 Prep: 6 hours and 10 minutes
Active: 30 minutes

 Serves 2–4

1. In a large pot, add all the brine ingredients. Bring to a boil, stir, and dissolve all sugar and salt. Remove from the heat and let cool completely. Add the brine to a large resealable bag or container, place the chicken in the brine, seal or cover, place in the fridge and brine for 4 hours.

2. Remove the chicken from the brine, wash off the brine, and pat the drumsticks dry, then set aside. In a medium bowl, whisk together the mirin, coconut palm sugar, pineapple juice, orange marmalade, sake, soy sauce, minced garlic, and ginger. If you would like less fat on your parrot, then remove the skin from the drumsticks before cooking. Heat the oil in a cast-iron pan over medium heat. Add the drumsticks and brown on all sides, about 2 minutes per side, moving occasionally to make sure they do not stick.

3. Add the sauce and coat the chicken completely. Reduce the heat to medium–low, cover the pan, and cook for 12 minutes. Remove the lid and flip the chicken. Turn the heat to high to get the sauce boiling and reducing down. Continue to flip chicken occasionally until it has reached an internal temperature of 170°F and the sauce is almost gone, about 7–8 minutes. Serve with napkins and try not to burn down the ship.

INGREDIENTS

Brine
- 1 gallon water
- 1 cup brown sugar
- ½ cup kosher (flaky) salt
- ½ cup soy sauce
- 2 cups apple cider vinegar
- 2 tsp peppercorns
- 2 large bay leaves

Chicken
- 2–2 ½ lbs chicken drumsticks
- 2 tbsp mirin
- 1 tbsp coconut palm sugar
- 3 tbsp pineapple juice
- 2 tbsp orange marmalade
- 1 tbsp sake
- 2 tbsp low-sodium soy sauce
- 1 tsp minced garlic
- 1 tsp grated ginger
- 1 tbsp coconut oil

BLACKENED DEVILFISH

This dish feels as though it came directly from the mouth of the volcano, and honestly, no other preparation of the regional Devilfish would do it justice.

 Easy　　 **Prep:** 20 minutes **Active:** 20 minutes　　 Serves 2–4　　 Pescatarian

1. Combine all the spices in a small bowl to make the rub. Cover the 4 dry fish fillets with the rub and let stand for 5 minutes.

2. Heat the oil in a cast-iron skillet on medium heat. Sear each fillet for 3 minutes on each side. Serve with limes and Charred Corn Salad.

INGREDIENTS

- 1 tsp each: garlic powder, onion powder, ground ginger, mango powder, smoked paprika and tomato powder
- ½ tsp each: dried oregano, chipotle powder, guajillo powder, salt

- 4 orange roughy fillets
- 1 tbsp coconut oil
- Limes

CHARRED CORN SALAD

1. Grill the corn and allow to cool. In a large bowl, toss the cilantro, onion, both tomatoes, lime juice, vinegar, olive oil, and salt. Set aside or in the fridge for 1 hour.

2. Mix the dressing ingredients. Mix and set aside. Slice the corn kernels carefully off cob and add to the bowl. Mix together. Serve with the dressing, with some avocado and cotija cheese.

INGREDIENTS

- 6 ears (cobs) of corn
- ¼ cup cilantro (coriander), chopped
- ¼ medium red onion, sliced
- ¼ cup sundried tomatoes, sliced
- ½ cup roma (plum) tomatoes, diced
- 1 tbsp lime juice
- 2 tbsp rice wine vinegar

- 1 tbsp olive oil
- ¼ tsp salt
- 1 avocado
- Cotija cheese (or feta cheese), crumbled

Dressing

- ¼ cup Mexican crema or sour cream
- ¼ cup mayonnaise
- 1 tbsp lime juice
- 1 tbsp cilantro, chopped
- 2 garlic cloves, minced
- ¼ tsp guajillo and chipotle powders
- 1 tsp lime zest

GRILLED KRAKEN TENTACLES

There are two sea posts in the Devil's Roar, of which Roaring Traders is by far the closest to Morrow's Peak. But for some pirates, who've weathered the angry volcanos and have also tangled with a Kraken, that extra half nautical mile might as well be a hundred. Tallulah graciously pays good gold to take that Kraken off their hands and turn it into this tasty, tender, grilled masterpiece.

 Easy   **Prep:** 20 minutes **Active:** 1 hour   Serves 6   Pescatarian

1. Combine the mirin, agave, vinegar, sake, soy sauce, and lime juice, then whisk in the garlic and ginger. Marinate the octopus for at least 30 minutes, but no longer than 2 hours.
2. Preheat an outdoor grill for medium-high heat and oil the grate to prevent sticking. Grill the octopus until charred on both sides, 3–4 minutes per side. Remove from the heat and place on a serving platter. Drizzle with Orange-Infused Olive Oil and squeeze lemon over the top. Season with salt and pepper. Serve immediately.

INGREDIENTS

- 2 tbsp mirin
- 1 tbsp agave syrup
- 2 tbsp rice wine vinegar
- 1 tbsp sake
- 1 tbsp low sodium soy sauce
- 2 tbsp lime juice
- 3 lbs pre-cooked octopus legs
- 1 tsp minced garlic
- 1 in piece fresh ginger, peeled and grated
- Orange-Infused Olive Oil (see page 12)
- 1 lemon
- Salt and pepper

ASHEN LAVA CAKE

The fiery glow of lava flowing through crevices and caverns was Tallulah's inspiration for this ashen dessert. She simply had to make something molten.

 Moderate

 Prep: 15 minutes
Active: 45 minutes

 Serves 4

 Vegetarian

1. Preheat the oven to 450°F. Butter and lightly flour four 7-oz ramekins. In a large mixing bowl, using an electric mixer and a whisk attachment, whisk the sugar, salt, extracts, and egg yolks together till very light in color and thick, and set aside. In a medium bowl, whisk the egg whites into stiff peaks. Set aside.

2. In a double boiler, melt the chocolate with ½ cup butter. Cool slightly then fold the chocolate into the sugar mixture. Fold in the flour, orange zest, and whipped egg whites. Pour chocolate cake mixture into floured ramekins up to about ¾ of the way up. Place on cookie sheet and bake for 13–15 minutes, or until outside crust forms and inside is still slightly jiggly. Remove and let stand for 3 minutes.

3. Taking care and using gloves or a dishtowel, stabilize the ramekins and, with a butter knife work, around the edge to dislodge the cake. Place a plate over the ramekin and invert it. Tap the bottom of the ramekin and carefully lift the ramekin, revealing the cake. Serve immediately, dusted with black sugar, and topped with whipped cream.

INGREDIENTS

- ¼ cup sugar
- ⅛ tsp sea salt
- ½ tsp orange extract
- ½ tsp vanilla extract
- 4 egg yolks
- 2 egg whites
- 6 oz bittersweet chocolate
- ½ cup butter, plus extra for greasing ramekins
- 2 tbsp flour
- 1 tsp orange zest
- Black sugar sprinkles
- Whipped cream, to serve

DEVIL'S SHROUD CAKE

Pirates voyaging into the crimson mist of the Devil's Shroud must equip the Shroudbreaker, lest they suffer a most tragic and fateful end.

 Moderate   **Prep:** 20 minutes
Inactive: 1 hour
Active: 1 hour   Serves 8   Vegetarian

1. Make sure all the ingredients are at room temperature and the butter and solid oils are softened. Preheat the oven to 325°F. Line two 8-inch cake pans with circles of parchment paper in the bottoms and spray the sides. Set aside. Whisk the flour, baking soda, and salt together in a large bowl. Set aside. In a stand mixer with a paddle attachment, cream the butter, add the sugar, and continue mixing on high speed for 3–4 minutes until combined. Add the oil and continue to mix until light and creamy, scraping the sides of the bowl. Add the eggs, 1 at a time, and process till combined. Sift in the cocoa powder carefully and mix completely.
2. In a small bowl, whisk together vinegar, extracts, and food coloring, using as much food coloring as needed to get the desired color. Add the red mixture to the sugar and eggs, making sure to mix completely. Remove the bowl from stand mixer and fold in the buttermilk and dry ingredients a third at a time until just combined. Do not overmix.
3. Transfer batter evenly to the prepared pans and bake for 30–32 minutes until a cake tester inserted in the center comes out almost clean. Remove from oven and cool completely. When ready to frost, slice off domed tops and set aside. Frost cake and sprinkle with crushed rock sugar and crumbled tops. Place in refrigerator to set frosting.

Frosting

1. In a stand mixer, cream the cream cheese and butter together until smooth, about 1–2 minutes. Add the powdered sugar and coconut milk a little at a time and mix on low speed until incorporated, then increase speed and beat for 2 minutes. Add the extracts, cornstarch, and salt and beat again. Transfer frosting to fridge for 20 minutes.

INGREDIENTS

- 3 cups flour
- 1 tsp baking soda
- 1 tsp salt
- ½ cup unsalted butter
- 1 ½ cups granulated sugar
- 1 cup coconut oil
- 2 eggs
- 2 tbsp unsweetened cocoa powder
- 3 tsp distilled white vinegar
- 1 tsp vanilla extract
- 1 tsp coconut extract
- 2 tbsp red liquid food coloring
- 1 cup buttermilk

Frosting

- 2 (8 oz) packages cream cheese
- ½ cup plant-based butter
- 4 cups powdered sugar
- 2–3 tbsp coconut milk
- 1 tsp vanilla extract
- 1 tsp coconut extract
- 2 tbsp cornstarch (flour)
- Pinch of salt
- Orange rock sugar, crushed

PIÑA COLAVA

Tallulah has been working on this grogtail for what seems like forever, but finally, it doesn't burn through the tankard. Although you best drink it fast, because I'm not so sure how she timed it.

1. In a drink mixer, combine the lime juice, rum, mango juice, and coconut water. Add ice cubes. Shake well until fully blended.

2. Pour into cocktail glass with or without ice. Pour the pomegranate liqueur into the glass over the back of a spoon. Garnish with a tajin-coated pineapple wedge. Enjoy while running from a volcano!

INGREDIENTS

- 1 oz fresh lime juice
- 1 oz good dark rum
- 2 oz mango juice
- 1 oz coconut water
- 1 tbsp pomegranate liqueur
- Tajin
- Pineapple wedge

S2OT

Refreshing hydration with just a hint of pineapple, all while staving off scurvy. Ice optional.

1. Combine all the ingredients in a large jug, stir, and bottle up for those long sea voyages.

INGREDIENTS

- 8 oz coconut water
- 4 oz pineapple juice
- 2 oz lime juice

SEA POSTS AND THE UNCHARTED

Across the Sea of Thieves there are a myriad of wondrous locations that a pirate may find refuge in, with only one not accessible by all who want to enter. The Sea Posts are small outposts that dot the seas, are open to all who have limited trade needs, and are the home of Chef Hendrick's and Merrick's Hunter's Call Trading Company. Here is where pirates come to trade in fish, meat, shark, and Kraken for precious gold, and where tavern-keepers and aspiring chefs come to buy it.

Other landmarks are not as easy to find, like the uncharted rock that is home to **The Glorious Sea Dog Tavern**. It's not visible on any map, but the aroma of their grilled Shadow Stormfish might have had you setting a direct course. Many a pirate used to find the courage after a few grogtails to take on the parkour course—it's a challenge even without the refreshments.

The truly uncharted is where all pirates eventually frequent an establishment like no other, hidden, secret, and legendary. **The Tavern of Legends** isn't on any map, it's in all places, all the time, and only accessible by those pirates who have lived and pirated long enough to become legends themselves. Sometimes, though, there is a faint aroma of properly cooked Barnacles in many of the taverns that makes a pirate long for the day the title Pirate Legend is finally earned.

THE GLORIOUS SEA DOG

Other taverns that dot the Sea of Thieves are in regions not always charted or accessible to all. Take, for example, The Glorious Sea Dog tavern. It was the headquarters of the Sea Dogs Trading Company, and it existed just south of K9 on the Sea of Thieves map. It was a large rock island, dead center to the main three regions that is not even a nautical mile from the Reaper's Hideout. There used to be a Pirate Arena on the island, but alas that is no more and the tavern's mascot, DeMarco's' dog Leopoldo, has long since wandered off somewhere.

The Glorious Sea Dog was run by Tilly. I wanted to get another taste of some of her best dishes, so I went to see Hendrick and he passed along all the recipes Tilly used to specialize in, all of which I share with you now. From the Grilled Shadow Stormfish to the Fiery Reaper's Coconut Curry Soup, Tilly certainly catered to regional pirates. But some of her best concoctions came to us as grogtails. The Salty Sea Dog Grog is a tasty treat, and if you plan on taking on the parkour route, then Tilly's Jump Challenge Boost is essential fuel for even the bravest of pirate runners.

SEA DOG TIKKA MASALA

Stories of mutinous crews on pirate ships abound, but the tale of the Seaward Glimmer is a culinary one, for it seems breadfruit trees were the commissioned cargo. On their quest to transport the trees from Mermaids Hideaway to Marauder's Arch, the crew grew angrier as the skies turned darker, and the water scarcer, igniting a mutiny which landed all the breadfruit trees in the drink, save for the few that were saved by the Sea Dogs.

 Easy
 Prep: 15 minutes
Active: 30–40 minutes
 Serves 4
 Vegan

1. Trim the breadfruit and batata, and chop into 1-inch pieces. In a large pot, bring salted water to a boil, add the breadfruit and batata, and parboil for 5 minutes. Remove, drain, and set aside.
2. Switch on the oven broiler. Cut the ginger and onion in half, cut the tomatoes in 4, and smash the garlic. Lay on a cookie sheet and place under the broiler (grill) until charred and fragrant. Remove and set aside.

(continued on next page)

INGREDIENTS

- 2 cups batata or
  Caribbean yam
- 2 cups breadfruit
- 4 cloves of garlic
- 2-inch piece root ginger, peeled
- 1 medium red onion
- 4 ripe plum tomatoes
- ½ tsp cumin
- ½ tsp turmeric
- ½ tsp ground cinnamon
- 2 tsp paprika
- 2 tsp garam masala

- 2 large chipotle peppers in adobo
- 1 x 15-oz can tomato sauce
- ½ cup fresh
  cilantro (coriander)
- 2 tbsp of coconut oil
- 1 cup plain coconut yogurt
- 1 x 13-oz can coconut cream
- 1 ripe mango, peeled and diced
- 1 x 15-oz can chickpeas,
  drained and rinsed
- ½ tsp salt

3. Add the spices to a dry pan and toast on low until fragrant, about 30 seconds. In a blender, add the peeled, roasted garlic, half the charred onion, ginger, and tomatoes, the chipotle peppers, tomato sauce, and cilantro. Blend until smooth. Add the spices and blend again. Dice the other half of the charred onion and add to a very large sauté pan with the coconut oil. Cook till translucent. Add the parboiled breadfruit and batata, and brown for a few minutes. Add the tomato mixture, yogurt, and half the coconut cream. Mix and bring to a boil. Reduce heat to a simmer and cook for 10 minutes. Add the chickpeas, the rest of the coconut milk, mango, and salt, combine and cook for another five minutes. Serve with white rice.

SHADOW STORMFISH

The area around this mountainous rock is a prime location to catch the elusive Shadow Stormfish, worth a king's ransom at any sea post, but best used by Tilly on the grill.

 Easy **Prep:** 10 minutes **Inactive:** 6–24 hours **Active:** 20 minutes Serves 4 Pescatarian

1. In a small bowl, whisk all ingredients except the fish, black pepper and salt. Add the swordfish steaks to a resealable plastic bag or to a shallow baking dish. Add the marinade, making sure swordfish is covered. Seal or cover with plastic wrap and place in the refrigerator. Marinate for 6 hours or overnight.
2. When ready to grill, remove the steaks from refrigerator and bring to room temperature. Scrape off and discard excess marinade. Oil the grill grate so the swordfish does not stick. Place steaks on grill and cook for 5–6 minutes per side. Transfer to a plate and allow to rest for 3 minutes before serving. Finish with ground pepper and salt. Serve with Flameheart's Charred Salsa.

INGREDIENTS

- 2 tbsp rice wine vinegar
- 2 tbsp mirin
- 1 tbsp soy sauce
- 1 tbsp Worcestershire sauce
- 1 tbsp agave syrup
- 3 tsp minced garlic
- 1 tbsp lemon zest
- 1 tbsp minced parsley
- ½ tsp red pepper flakes
- 4 x 8-oz swordfish steaks
- Freshly ground black pepper
- Flaky sea salt

FLAMEHEART'S CHARRED SALSA

 Easy **Prep:** 20 minutes **Active:** 10-15 minutes Varies Vegan

1. Oil the grill grate and over semi-direct heat grill the tomatoes and jalapeno, turning frequently to make sure all sides are charred. Remove and allow to cool.
2. In the meantime, peel and core the mango and char for a few minutes until the surface is caramelized. Remove from grill and set aside. Peel off the charred skin, core and deseed the tomatoes and jalapeno. Dice the tomato, jalapeno, onions, and mango and add to a bowl with the lime juice, cilantro, and salt.

INGREDIENTS

- 3 roma (plum) tomatoes
- ½ jalapeno
- 1 ripe mango
- ¼ cup white onion
- ¼ cup red onion
- 2 tbsp cilantro (coriander), chopped
- Juice of 1 lime
- Salt

REAPER'S BONES CHICKEN COCONUT SOUP

This dish is a Reaper's favorite meal on long cold voyages across uncharted waters. Its ingredients hit the right balance needed to keep a sharp eye out for fluttering Alliance flags and just like those who sail for The Reaper's Bones, the broth is warming, but can sneak up on you with blazing heat. Warning: red flags spotted on the horizon.

 Easy

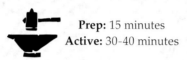 **Prep:** 15 minutes
Active: 30-40 minutes

 Serves 4

This soup can be made VEGAN by removing the chicken, replacing chicken stock with vegetable stock and fish sauce with coconut aminos.

1. Cut the potatoes, turnip, and carrots into small, equal-sized cubes and set aside. Trim and slice the lemongrass stalk into 2-inch strips and set aside. Cut the chicken thighs into strips. In a small fry pan, add 1 tbsp coconut oil and brown the chicken strips, around 4–5 minutes.

2. In the meantime, in a Dutch oven or a medium soup pot, add 1 tbsp coconut oil and the red Thai curry paste. Fry gently till aromatic, about 30 seconds. Add the leek and 1 tsp salt and fry for another 2 minutes. Add the ginger and combine. Cook for 1 minute.

3. Add all the veggies, the chilis, lemongrass, 2 tsp salt, stir, and cook for another 2 minutes. Add all the liquids and the browned chicken, stir, and bring to a boil. Reduce the heat to simmer and cook uncovered for 15–20 minutes until the vegetables are tender. Remove from heat and add lime juice and the basil. Serve with extra limes and fresh basil. Note: if Ancientscale fish sauce is not available, any fish sauce will work perfectly.

INGREDIENTS

- 2 small potatoes
- 2 carrots
- 1 turnip
- 1 lemongrass stalk
- 3 chicken thighs, skin and bone removed
- 2 tbsp coconut oil
- 1 tbsp red Thai curry paste
- 1 cup leek, sliced
- 1 tbsp ginger, grated
- 3 Thai chilis, seeded and chopped
- 3 cups low sodium chicken stock
- 3 cups coconut milk
- ¼ cup cream of coconut
- 2 tbsp Ancientscale fish sauce or coconut aminos
- 3 tbsp lime juice
- 3 tsp kosher salt (flaky sea salt)
- 1 tbsp chopped basil
- Limes

JUMP CHALLENGE BOOST

Need to get across that parkour course in one piece? Say no more, Tilly has the concoction that will put that boost in your peg leg and get you to the top.

1. Add the coconut pulp and ice to a rocks glass. In a drink shaker, add the ginger, sugar, turmeric, and lime juice.
2. Using a muddler, mash together the ingredients at the bottom. Add in ice, the coconut water, and mango juice. Shake to blend, strain into glass. Garnish with crystallized ginger.

INGREDIENTS

- 1 tbsp coconut pulp
- 3 slices fresh ginger
- ½ tsp coconut palm sugar
- ¼ tsp ground turmeric
- 1 oz lime juice
- 3 oz mango juice
- 4 oz coconut water
- Crystallized ginger

SALTY SEA DOG GROG

As grogtails go, Tilly essentially struck gold with this blend.
It's perfectly tart, sweet, and salty.

1. Set up plate with sea salt. Moisten the rim of a glass or tankard with a lime wedge and coat the rim with salt. In a drink mixer, add the sugar and grapefruit juice, mixing well to dissolve the sugar.
2. Add ice cubes, the rum, and coconut water. Shake well and pour over ice.

INGREDIENTS

- Sea salt
- Wedge of lime
- 2 tsp brown sugar
- 2 oz grapefruit juice
- 2 oz rum
- 2 oz coconut water

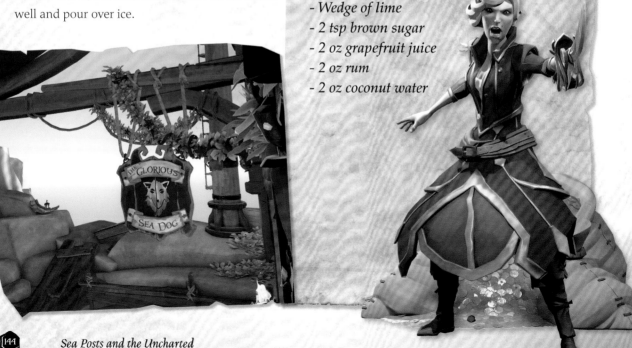

THE TAVERN OF LEGENDS

One of the most famous taverns in the Sea of Thieves happens to also be one of the most secretive, and certainly not accessible to all pirates. Only those that have attained Pirate Legend status have access to it, as it lives within the Pirate Legend Hideout. The Tavern of Legends is home to the Pirate Lord himself, as well as a handful of dearly departed pirates that have traversed the Sea of Thieves and now inhabit the Athena's Fortune ship hull. Legendary Louise is the bartender here, and although she's never been inclined to sell grog or food, since the current tavern rats would gain no benefit from either, Chef Hendrick did assist in developing a legendary menu for visiting pirates who fancy a spirited grogtail or some aptly named pub fare.

While here, Chef Hendrick was able to convince his brother Merrick to give Louise his recipe for Whale's Tail and Chips–it was his specialty on the Killer Whale, and it's now a tavern staple and a pirate classic. But one of the most visually stunning menu items has got to be the blended drink inspired by Merrick's famed Megalodon tale, the tale of the Shrouded Ghost. This drink may inspire you to drop a few gold pieces on the bar and immediately set sail, trolling the seas. Before you leave, though, enjoy some shanties as performed by the ghostly crew of the Killer Whale, and make sure you hear the latest joke from Blind Bob–a good belly laugh is great for digestion.

MERRICK'S WHALE'S TAIL AND SOT CHIPS

At long last, Merrick has joined his Killer Whale crew here in the Tavern of Legends. It seems fitting that he shares his splashtail recipe with Legendary Louise so that all Pirate Legends may enjoy this moist and flaky meal that only the Killer Whale crew were once able to savor. Louise starts preparing this dish a couple of days ahead so that it's ready just about the time you're back from your Thieves' Haven run.

 Moderate

 Prep: 20 minutes
Inactive: 2–24 hours+
Active: 20 minutes

 Serves 2–4

 Pescatarian

INGREDIENTS

- 2–3 cups vegetable oil
- 4 cod fillets
- 1 cup + 1 tbsp flour
- 3 tbsp cornstarch (cornflour)
- 1 tsp baking powder
- ⅓ cup light Caribbean lager or stout
- ⅓ cup ginger beer
- ⅓ cup seltzer (sparkling) water
- 2 tsp salt

SoT Chips
- 4 russet potatoes
- 1 tbsp cornstarch (cornfour)
- 6 cups canola (rapeseed) oil
- Coconut vinegar/malt
  vinegar 50:50 blend
- Granulated crystallized lime
- Salt

Special equipment: French fry cutter or potato slicer

1. Heat the oil in a deep pan over medium heat to 350°F. Slice the fillets into 2 pieces. Salt the fish lightly with 1 tsp salt. Dust them with 1 tbsp flour. Combine all the dry ingredients and 1 tsp salt in a mixing bowl. Whisk in the stout or lager, ginger beer, and seltzer water until all lumps are gone and the batter has a smooth consistency.

2. Dip the fish in the batter and then place in the oil. Fry for 4–5 minutes until golden brown. Continue to flip until golden and crispy. Set aside on paper towels to drain.

SoT Chips

1. This process should happen a day or more ahead of time. The potatoes can go into the freezer after Step 3. Peel the potatoes and, using a potato slicer, make potato fries. *(continued on next page)*

Soak them in a cold-water bath for 30 minutes. Drain the potatoes, then lay on a rack to dry out for 20 minutes.

2. Add the cornstarch to a large bowl, and toss the potatoes. Shake off excess cornstarch and set the potatoes aside for 20 minutes.

3. Using an oil or candy (sugar) thermometer, heat the oil in a deep pan to 325°F. Lower the potatoes into the oil and fry for 5 minutes. Transfer to a cooling rack over a cookie sheet for 15 minutes. At this point you can let them cool completely and freeze them.

4. When ready to serve, if frozen, you can either heat them in an oven at 450°F for 10–15 minutes or follow the next step. Heat the oil in a deep pan to 375°F, add fries directly into oil and fry for 3–5 minutes until golden brown and crispy. Remove from oil and drain on paper towels. Season with salt, crystalized lime juice, and the coconut/malt vinegar mix.

BARNACLES WITH GARLIC

The hull in Athena's Fortune Hideout collects many barnacles throughout the days. Keeping it clean, as it so happens, is a rather savory and delicious endeavor. I'm not sure if they put something in the water down here, but the garlicked barnacles are the best I have ever tasted.

 Easy   **Prep:** 10 minutes **Active:** 15 minutes   Serves 2–4   Seafood

INGREDIENTS

- 1 tbsp butter
- 1 tbsp coconut oil
- ½ cup leek, thinly sliced
- 2 garlic cloves, finely chopped
- ½ cup chicken stock
- ½ cup dry sake
- 2 lbs mussels, cleaned

- 1 tbsp coconut milk
- 1 tbsp coconut cream
- ¼ tsp sea salt
- 1 tbsp fresh parsley, roughly chopped
- Salt and fresh ground black pepper
- Lemon wedges, to serve
- 1 baguette, warmed, to serve

1. In a large Dutch oven over medium-high heat, melt the butter and coconut oil. When melted and bubbling, add the leek and garlic. Stir and cook for 2 minutes. Add the chicken stock, sake, and mussels and give a good mix.

2. Cover the pot and steam for 7–10 minutes until all the mussels have opened. If any mussels do not open, discard them. Meanwhile, combine the coconut milk and cream together to get a thick coconut milk and set aside. After mussels have opened, remove the pot from the heat, move the mussels to one side in the pot and add the coconut mixture, salt, and parsley to the broth, and stir. Taste the broth and adjust to taste with salt and pepper.

3. Move the mussels back to the broth and toss, covering the mussels. Serve in big bowls with lemon wedges and a crusty baguette to sop up the broth.

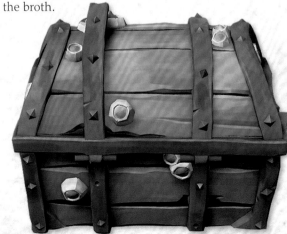

PIRATE LORD SALAD

With the combination of green fruits, green vegetables, and crunchy nuts, all in a sweet and savory dressing that surrounds each piece like an aura, it's easy to see why the Pirate Lord insisted on this salad being his namesake. He also really likes tiny marshmallows in it.

Enjoy as you contemplate the Pirate Lord's words: "For what is the Sea of Thieves but a haven for those with adventure in their hearts and mischief in their souls!"

 Easy   **Prep:** 15 minutes
Active: 10 minutes   Serves 8   Vegetarian

1. Core and dice up the apples into bite-size pieces, add to a large bowl with lemon juice, and toss. Dice the celery and add to the bowl. Slice the grapes into 3 or 4 slices per grape. Add them to the bowl. Sprinkle with sugar and toss together. Add the pineapple chunks and give another toss.

2. Roughly chop the nuts and add them to the bowl, then toss. In a medium bowl, using an electric hand mixer, whip the cream and coconut extract until thick. Fold in the mayo until thoroughly combined. Add the whipped cream mixture to the fruit and fold together. Slice the bananas into ¼-inch rounds and fold into mixture along with the marshmallows. Cover bowl and refrigerate the salad for 2 hours or overnight. When ready to serve, add the toasted coconut and toss.

INGREDIENTS

- 2 cups green apple
- 1 tbsp lemon juice
- 3 stalks celery
- 1 cup green seedless grapes
- 1 tbsp white sugar
- 1 cup pineapple chunks
- ¼ cup toasted unsalted macadamia nuts
- ¼ cup toasted pistachios
- ½ cup heavy whipping cream
- ½ tsp coconut extract
- ¼ cup Homemade Mayo (see page 11)
- 2 ripe bananas
- 1 cup tiny marshmallows
- ¼ cup toasted shredded coconut

BELLE'S ENCHANTED LANTERN

With its green ghostly glow and crisp cool taste, this cocktail harkens back to Belle's illuminating light helping guide courageous pirates through challenging adventures. Raise your glass up and see what you've been missing.

1. Add the crème de menthe, crème de coconut, cream, and light rum to a drink mixer with ice. Shake well.
2. Pour over one large ice cube in a rocks glass. Top off with Goldschläger.

INGREDIENTS

- ½ oz crème de menthe
- 1 oz crème de coconut
- 1 oz cream
- 1 oz light rum
- ½ oz Goldschläger

SHROUDED GHOST

Like the elusive beast that is the Shrouded Ghost, this drink has all the markings you longingly look for as you trawl the seas: White and pink streaks with those ghostly red eyes. Some say it's all a tall tale, there is no Shrouded Ghost, but Merrick knows better, and deep down so do you.

1. Pour the grenadine into a goblet and place in the freezer for at least 15 minutes.

2. When ready to serve, add all the other ingredients except the pomegranate seeds to a blender and process on liquify for 1 minute. Remove the goblet from freezer and tilt and swirl the goblet, coating the sides of the glass with the cold grenadine. Use the back of a spoon if needed.

3. Add the pomegranate juice, and then slowly add the blended mixture, taking care not to combine. Finish with the pomegranate seeds.

INGREDIENTS

- ½ oz grenadine
- 6 oz coconut milk
- 3 oz cream of coconut
- 1 banana
- ½ tsp vanilla
- 3 oz pomegranate juice
- 1 tbsp pomegranate seeds

DIETARY NOTES

The tavern galleys have all the best ingredients that can be found in the Sea of Thieves and beyond, but for some of you swashbuckling pirates these tasty foods can keep your ships docked, sails furled and wishing the Ferryman comes sooner than later. Fear not, pirate, for this culinary journal is much more of a map, with destinations drawn, treasures marked, yet with many courses still to be set.

For lactose-intolerant scallywags, you might have noticed that this journal is mostly made up of coconut milk, for it is plentiful on the islands. So fear not. And where recipes call for cheese, or actual dairy products, the Merchants always have dairy-free options that can easily be substituted.

Altering any of the recipes to your taste is simple, but takes a skilled hand, for changing course mid-quest requires a bit of adapting. Anything in this journal can be made vegan with easy swaps; vegetable stock for chicken, plant butter for regular, coconut or almond milk for regular and vegan egg for chicken. Take care, for each change that is made requires some minor updates to cooking times and possibly even the amount of ingredients.

So where's the Shark?
Where are the Megs?

Ah yes, you are a keenly observant pirate indeed. This journal documents recipes from across the Sea of Thieves in the wake of Chef Hendrick's legendary quest to make this magical world a culinary haven. In this world, Megalodons are sighted often and sharks, well, they easily find their way into a galley's pan. But in the wider world these creatures are scarce, endangered, and for one, extinct. Tavern-keepers take great care in what they serve on their menus, and this journal follows their example. If you are a pirate wanting to keep the sea brimming with fish and even those pesky sharks, then make your next quest one of ocean conservation and sustainability, and set course for https://www. seafoodwatch.org/ or https://www.mcsuk.org/ goodfishguide/

CULINARY CONVERSIONS

VOLUME

IMPERIAL	CUPS	METRIC
	¼ tsp	1.25 ml
	¼ tsp	2.5 ml
	1 tsp	5 ml
	1 tbsp	15 ml
3 ½ fl oz		100 ml
4 ½ fl oz	½ cup	125 ml
5 fl oz		150 ml
7 fl oz		200 ml
9 fl oz	1 cup	250 ml
11 fl oz		300 ml
14 fl oz		400 ml
18 fl oz	2 cups	500 ml
26 fl oz	3 cups	750 ml
35 fl oz	4 cups	1L
53 fl oz	6 cups	1.5L
70 fl oz	8 cups	2L

WEIGHT

IMPERIAL	METRIC
½ oz	15g
1 oz	30g
2 oz	60g
3 oz	85g
4 oz (½lb)	115g
5 oz	140g
6 oz	170g
7 oz	200g
8 oz (½lb)	230g
16 oz (1lb)	450g
32 oz (2 lb)	450g
35 oz (2 ½ lb)	1kg

TEMPERATURE

FAHRENHEIT	CELSIUS	GAS
250°F	120°C	½
275°F	140°C	1
300°F	150°C	2
325°F	160°C	3
350°F	180°C	4
375°F	190°C	5
400°F	200°C	6
425°F	220°C	7
450°F	230°C	8
475°F	240°C	9
500°F	260°C	10

RECIPE LISTS

ABOUT THE AUTHOR

SHREDZ N' BIXBY

Kayce Baker is a photographer and marketer by trade and a chef by design. She's a gamer, a streamer, and a girl who ate her first coconut at the age of four. With her culinary roots entrenched in Latin cuisine, she embraces rich and flavorful recipes that aspire to brighten every meal. Kayce is a cookbook author, cat lover, scuba diver, angler, virtual pub owner, content creator, snowboarder, archer, tequila expert, aspiring Aston Martin owner, and the wearer of a Left Shark onesie. When she's not off on worldly adventures with Bob, experimenting in the kitchen, editing videos, or binge-watching some new horror show, she can be found at twitch.tv/elgatopub, pirating and streaming *Sea of Thieves* as Shredz.

ACKNOWLEDGMENTS

By the Author

Thankful doesn't come close to what I feel for all these amazing human beings. To Bob, for being my life, my love, and my taste tester. To Victoria Rosenthal, Pixelated Vicka–you are an inspiration, your talent and generosity are legend. I created many of my own props but for those I did not, I called in special help from the following artists: Daniel Dziubinski from Tentacle Creations, Elizabeth Burton from lizalaroo artstation, Chloe Palmer from ChloeSaurusCrafts, CaptDrasuk, and Wandering Wastelander. Thank you to Soycha Art for my SOT character and cat portrait. And, of course, huge thanks to all the Gatos from our little Gato Pub community for being the best bunch of scallywags anyone can ever ask for.

By Rare

Special thanks to Peter Hentze, Adam Park, Chris Allcock, Shiying Li, Isher Dhillon, Allen Namiq, Anna Collins, Mike Chapman, David Ferguson, David Rammell, Cliff Thomas, Brendan Smith, Garry Thomas, and Linda Cox.